The Grace of God and the Grace of Man

THE THEOLOGIES OF BRUCE SPRINGSTEEN

Azzan Yadin-Israel

Lingua Press
700 South First Avenue
Highland Park, NJ 08904

Author photo by Mary Laurano
Book Layout ©2013 BookDesignTemplates.com

The Grace of God and the Grace of Man: The Theologies of Bruce Springsteen/ Azzan Yadin-Israel. —1st ed.
ISBN 978-0-6927185-1-3

To A., who ran sad and ran free

Contents

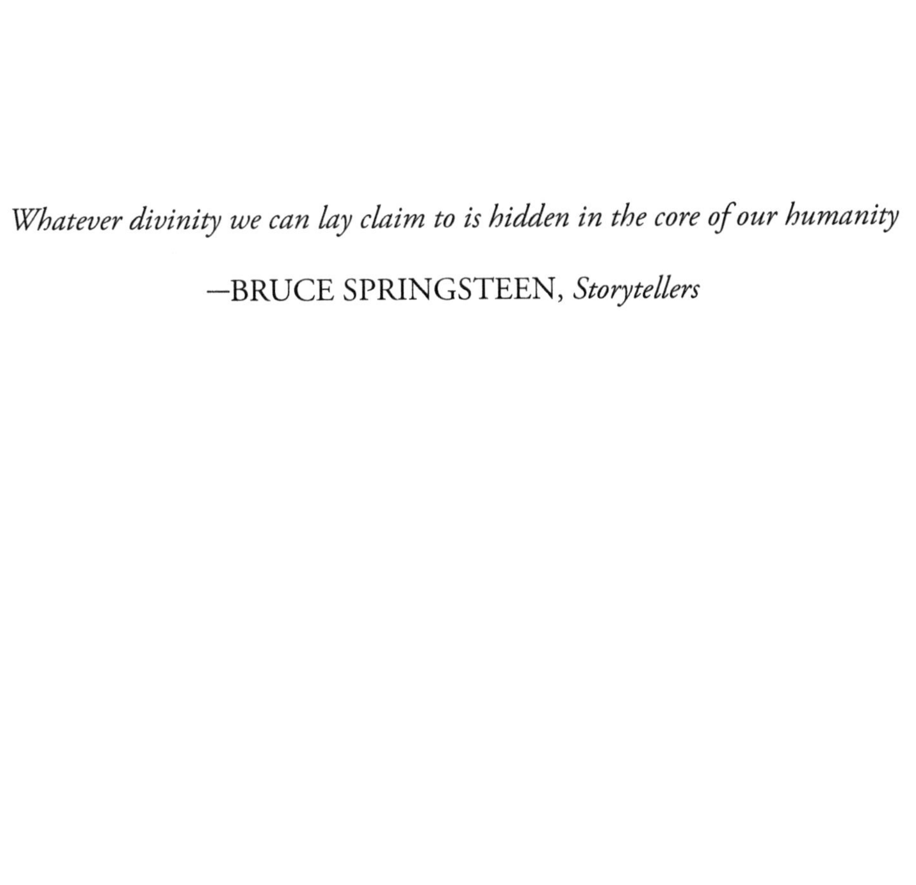

Whatever divinity we can lay claim to is hidden in the core of our humanity

—BRUCE SPRINGSTEEN, *Storytellers*

INTRODUCTION

Biography and Theology

In his essay "The Spirit of Place," D. H. Lawrence famously wrote that readers should "never trust the artist. Trust the tale."[1] A number of writers have paraphrased this instruction, including Bruce Springsteen, when he says "[t]rust the art, be suspicious of the artist. He's generally untrustworthy himself."[2] In truth, some forms of art are easy to separate from the artists: the more theatrical, the more scripted a performance, the less observers tend to think of it as an expression of the artist's authentic self. Audiences expect singers headlining Las Vegas casinos to put on a show, but singer-songwriters are more closely

[1] D. H. Lawrence, "The Spirit of Place," in his *Studies in Classic American Literature*, Ezra Greenspan et al., editors, *The Cambridge Edition of the Works of D. H. Lawrence* (Cambridge: Cambridge University Press, 2003), 14.
[2] Quoted in Christopher Phillips and Louis P. Masur, *Talk About a Dream: The Essential Interviews of Bruce Springsteen* (New York: Bloomsbury, 2013), 11.

associated with their biographies. Our cultural understanding of Johnny Cash would be very different if he had written the same music while working as a corporate accountant and living comfortably in the suburbs.[3]

Bruce Springsteen's public persona, especially in the eyes of his fans, is located securely on the "authentic" side of this divide.[4] As a songwriter, his works often reflect elements from his life: struggles with his father, romantic triumphs and failures, the joys of fatherhood, as well as social issues that concern him. As a performer, Springsteen blurs the borders between his music and his personal life, delivering long onstage monologues about his youth, his family, his bandmates, and more.

In light of the overwhelming cultural association of Springsteen's artistic voice and his biographical self, it is important to emphasize at the outset that this book is about Bruce Springsteen's lyrics, not about Bruce Springsteen. Of course, Springsteen's lyrics are, in some sense, an expression of his thoughts, beliefs, and creativity. But it remains difficult and perhaps impossible to know whether or how much, precisely, a given song relates to Springsteen's personal beliefs. Numerous scholarly writers make the facile assumption that the "I" of a song's character is, for all intents and purposes, Springsteen himself—at least they do so when the character fits with what they assume to be Springsteen's own voice. Consider the song "Nebraska" from the album of the same name. No sane interpreter would argue that a first-person speaker unapologetically recalling his murderous rampage through Nebraska and Wyoming is a stand-in for Bruce Springsteen. Yet many listeners who would rightly scoff at any attempt to associate Springsteen with the character in "Nebraska," will insist that songs about grace or redemption are true expressions of Springsteen's inner self. My argument is not that they are *not*—I do not know Bruce Springsteen and

[3] For an excellent study of authenticity in country music see Maxine L. Grossman, "Jesus, Mama, and the Constraints on Salvific Love in Contemporary Country Music," *Journal of the American Academy of Religion* 70 (2002), 83-115; reprinted in Michael J. Gilmour, editor, *Call Me the Seeker: Listening to Religion in Popular Music* (New York and London: Continuum, 2005), 267-98.

[4] As William Wolff has shown, Springsteen himself has offered a nuanced discussion of authenticity that ultimately serves as a defense of the legitimacy of this concept and of his claim to it. See Wolff, "Springsteen, Tradition, and the Purpose of the Artist," *BOSS: The Biannual Online-Journal of Springsteen Studies* 1 (2014), 36-73.

could not in any case judge a song's biographical "authenticity"—but rather that his songs can and ought be examined primarily as literary works, divorced from the circumstances of their composition. In keeping with this approach, I use the term "singer" as a rough synonym of "narrator," denoting the character whose voice presents the events of a song (often in the first person). Following this convention, the man who left his wife and kids in Baltimore, the song's protagonist, is the singer of "Hungry Heart," not the artist performing the song.

One upshot of this approach is that this book does not focus on Springsteen's biography even when there are compelling commonalities between his early life and later artistic concerns. To cite one well-known example, fans and scholars alike draw a straight line from Springsteen's childhood in the blue-collar town of Freehold, NJ, to his songs extolling the dignity of working men and women.[5] But it is important to keep in mind that many musicians grew up in blue collar neighborhoods and towns, but their experience was not reflected in their art: the Beatles had their inception in Liverpool; Iggy Pop lived in a trailer park in Ypsilanti, Michigan; Celine Dion grew up the youngest of fourteen children, her mother a homemaker and her father a butcher. Yet none of them translated their childhood experience into core elements of their music, certainly not to the extent that Springsteen did.[6] Moreover, Springsteen himself did not always give these themes pride of place in his writing. His first two albums, *Greetings from Asbury Park, N.J.* and *The Wild, the Innocent & the E Street Shuffle*, hardly touch on blue-collar themes, while *Born to Run* and *Darkness on the Edge of Town* portray daily work as an oppressive activity, devoid of positive meaning.[7] So

[5] See the discussion in Bryan K. Garman, *A Race of Singers: Whitman's Working –Class Hero from Guthrie to Springsteen* (Chapel Hill and London: The University of North Carolina Press, 2000), 195-258; Jefferson Cowie and Lauren Boehm, "Dead Man's Town: 'Born in the U.S.A.,' Social History, and Working-Class Identity," *American Quarterly* 58 (2006), 353-78.

[6] Conversely, not all writers who address blue collar issues grew up in working-class families. Emma Lazarus, whose "New Colossus" may be the best-known American affirmation of the dignity of the poor ("Give me your tired, your poor/Your huddled masses yearning to breathe free") was born into an affluent Sephardic-Jewish family, read German, Italian, and French, and worked extensively on the poetry of Goethe. See Esther Schor, *Emma Lazarus* (New York: Knopf, 2006).

[7] See the discussion below, chapter two.

while Springsteen's blue-collar songs certainly draw on the experiences of his youth, they are not *determined* by these experiences and thus are not reducible to autobiography. For Springsteen (and other artists with similar backgrounds), engaging or avoiding blue-collar themes is an artistic choice, not a biographical compulsion.

The same reasoning guides my treatment of Springsteen's Catholicism, a prominent and too-often confused presence in discussions of the religious motifs in his work. In an early discussion of this subject, Father Andrew Greeley examines the preponderance of Christian and specifically Catholic images in Springsteen's music.[8] As the first essay (to my knowledge) to explicitly take up the theological dimension of Springsteen's work, Greely's insights have had an abiding influence on subsequent scholarship, particularly as regards the biographical determinism that informs Greeley's analysis. Springsteen's work, according to Greeley, reflects the Catholic imagery that surrounded him as a child:

> Catholicism is a religion rich with metaphor systems … It inundates the preconscious of its members very early in life with intensely powerful, pervasive, and durable images that shape the activity of the agent intellect for the rest of life … The preconscious is certainly Catholic by the time one is six and, arguably, after one's first conscious Christmas experience.[9]

The term *preconscious* refers to an aspect of the mind that precedes rational thought and provides the categories we use to make sense of the world around us—a "metaphor maker" that guides us in linking one received image to another.[10] By shifting the Catholic self away from the conscious mind and identifying it with the preconscious, Greeley lays the foundation for the claim that Springsteen's early exposure to Catholic imagery serves as the basis for his music, even if he (in his conscious

[8] Andrew Greeley, "The Catholic Imagination of Bruce Springsteen," *America* (February 6, 1988), 232-43; reprinted in June Skinner Sawyers, editor, *Racing in the Street: The Bruce Springsteen Reader* (New York: Penguin, 2004), 155-64.

[9] Greeley, "Catholic Imagination," 235.

[10] Greeley, "Catholic Imagination," 234.

mind) believes his inspiration lies elsewhere. Springsteen, Greeley claims, "engages in this 'minstrel ministry' without ever being explicit about it, or even necessarily aware of it."[11]

Setting aside Greeley's problematic psychological claims, his attempt to draw a direct line between the religious traditions of Springsteen's childhood and his adult life-choices is both too narrow and too broad. [12] The link is too narrow in its denial of later influence: spiritual journeys do not end when we reach the age of six; adult artists can encounter new views that inform and even transform their work. These views may contradict the traditions of their youth, or they may resonate with and enrich them, but in either case it impoverishes our understanding of the artist to shackle them to their childhood. Greeley's claim is too broad in that it posits a correspondence that in many cases cannot be justified: Mick Jagger, Paul McCartney, and Elvis Costello all grew up Catholic; both Sting and Johnny Rotten attended Catholic School through high school. According to Greeley, Catholicism should have been stamped into their preconscious and found expression in their music. But I suspect that the songs of the Beatles, the Rolling Stones, the Police, Sting (as a solo artist), the Sex Pistols, and Elvis Costello collectively contain fewer biblical allusions than Springsteen's songbook.[13] Moreover, Springsteen himself does not deal with religious and theological matters consistently. At certain points in his career he has produced lyrics that are on the whole free of explicit religious or biblical imagery. *Born in the U.S.A.*, for example, has little or no such imagery, though his childhood was no less Catholic when writing that album than when writing *The Rising*.

It is worth noting that Springsteen's estimation of the role of Catholicism in his work has varied dramatically over time. In an early interview with Robert Duncan, Springsteen states plainly: "I was raised Catholic and everybody who was raised Catholic hates religion ... I quit

---

[11] Greeley, "Catholic Imagination," 233.

[12] Greeley does not recognize the complexity and ambivalence of Springsteen's use of traditional images and, as a result, his claims that Springsteen is "a Catholic minstrel" and "a liturgist" (233) are overwrought. The lack of nuance may be due to Greeley's determination to cast Springsteen as "a superb example of why Catholics cannot leave the church" (233).

[13] Of course, some of these artists have written religiously-themed songs, such as the Paul McCartney-penned "Let It Be."

that stuff when I was in eighth grade. By the time you're older than thirteen it's too ludicrous to go along with anymore."[14] Forty years later, in a long, personal conversation with Elvis Costello, Springsteen offered a very different appreciation:

> It's a funny thing ... I look back and I've got a lot of harsh memories of my childhood. It was very strict religion at the time and blah, blah, blah. But at the same time, it was an epic canvas and it gave you a sense of revelation, retribution, perdition, bliss, ecstasy. When you think that that was being presented to you as a five- or six-year-old child ... I think I've been trying to write my way out of it ever since.[15]

Like his blue-collar background, Springsteen's Catholic upbringing informs his writing, and can illuminate the social and cultural setting of his formative years. But it is analytically inadequate to reduce his artistic expression to biographical terms.[16]

Indeed, there are compelling reasons to think that biographical considerations are fundamentally extrinsic to literary analysis as such, at least so long as we understand biography as the major relationships and events in a person's life.[17] For while it is clear that artists draw on

---

[14] Robert Duncan, "Lawdamercy, Springsteen Saves!" *Creem* (October 1978); reprinted in Jeff Burger, editor, *Springsteen on Springsteen: Interviews, Speeches, and Encounters* (Chicago: Chicago Review, 2013), 85.

[15] The interview is part of the *Spectacle: Elvis Costello with...* series, and appeared on the Sundance Channel on January 20th, 2010; reprinted in Phillips and Masur, *Talk About a Dream*, 379-80.

[16] The scholarly tendency toward deterministic interpretations of artists' youth is not limited to Springsteen. David Brown has recently written that "[Bob] Dylan is a Jew by parentage and also by early upbringing, and this no doubt explains the appearance of biblical allusions in his [early lyrics]" (David Brown, *God and Grace of Body: Sacrament in Ordinary* [Oxford and New York: Oxford University Press, 2007], 309). Since I can think of a good number of Jews who do not make a habit of alluding to the Bible, there is, in fact, quite a bit of doubt as to whether Dylan's parentage can explain his poetics. In a footnote to the above statement (n. 61), Brown substantiates his claim thus: "[Dylan] was born Robert Allen Zimmerman in 1941 and in 1954 he duly celebrated his bar mitzvah." There we have the sum total of Brown's evidence—Dylan's Jewish surname and bar mitzvah.

[17] The analytic separation of the artist and the work is a cornerstone of New Criticism (and several subsequent theoretical orientations), famously formulated in William K. Wimsatt and Monroe C. Beardsley, "The Intentional Fallacy," *Sewanee Review* 54 (1946), 468-88; revised and reprinted in Wimsatt and Monroe, *The Verbal Icon: Studies in the Meaning of Poetry* (Lexington: University of Kentucky Press, 1954), 3-18.

their experience, experience encompasses more than biography: it is the sum total of their memories, thoughts, imaginings, feelings, and so on. Childhood experiences are part of an artist's experience, but they are not (or, not necessarily) a privileged part—there is no reason to allot them more weight than the artist's social and political commitments, aesthetic preferences, imagined realities, and the like. Artists transform their experiences into art, and in this regard too, major life events are not more significant than other types of experience. Bruce Springsteen has stated explicitly that "The Wish" (*Tracks*) is about his mother purchasing him a guitar when he was sixteen, despite the family's difficult financial situation. Springsteen has also stated that the songs on *Nebraska* were inspired by the Charlie Starkweather killings, Howard Zinn's *A People's History of the United States*, and the stories of Flannery O'Connor, none of which are part of Springsteen's biography as the term is generally understood. In so far as we are interested in Springsteen as a songwriter, the distinction between biographical and non-biographical influences is immaterial, since the question is the same for (the biographical) "The Wish" and (the non-biographical) "Nebraska": how does Springsteen transform his experience into song?

Readers unconvinced by this argument, who still seek guidance from the author, should note that Springsteen himself seeks to distance his writing from his biographical self when he states that the work of the singer-songwriter "calls for the listener to take a step back and realize that they're listening to a creation of some sort, a work of imagination." Of course, Springsteen does not deny that writers are shaped by their biography, but

> to overpersonalize it is generally a mistake. As a writer you're paid to use your imagination, and your emotions, and your eyes, to create something that is real ... But because you come out on stage and sing in that voice and tell that story, it may make the lines a little greyer than with novelists or film directors—I don't think anyone thinks Martin Scorsese is *in* the Mafia![18]

[18] Interview with Patrick Humphries, *Record Collector* 1999; reprinted in Phillips and Masur, *Talk About a Dream*, 269.

Without denying the importance of biographical study on its own terms, the remainder of this introduction explores other approaches for the analysis of religious elements in Springsteen's lyrics.

Music and Religion

There is a significant body of scholarship that examines popular culture through the lens of religious studies—fan communities as religious congregations, dieting regimens as paths to salvation, sports heroes as modern-day saints and, of course, popular music.[19] Much of the work on music focuses on the experience of the audience, arguing that music is a site of ultimate meaning for many listeners.[20] Certainly, many of Springsteen's most ardent fans understand their relationship with his music in terms that draw heavily from the religious lexicon, as Daniel Cavicchi and Linda Randall have demonstrated.[21] In part, this quasi-religious orientation is a response to motifs that, though not strictly

[19] See Michael Jindra, "It's About Faith in Our Future: Star Trek Fandom as Cultural Religion," in Bruce David Forbes and Jeffrey H. Mahan, editors, *Religion and Popular Culture in America* (Berkeley and Los Angeles: University of California Press, 2005), 159-73; Michelle M. Lewica, "Losing Their Way to Salvation: Women, Weight Loss, and the Salvation Myth of Culture Lite," in Forbes and Mahan, *Religion and Popular Culture in America*, 174-94; Joseph L. Price, "An American Apotheosis: Sports as Popular Religion," in Forbes and Mahan, *Religion and Popular Culture in America*, 195-212.

[20] See Rupert Till, *Pop Cult: Religion and Popular Music* (London and New York: Continuum, 2010); Craig Detweiler, *A Matrix of Meanings: Finding God in Pop Culture* (Grand Rapids, MI: Baker Academic, 2003), 155-84. I have learned a great deal about the study of religion and popular music from Jonathan D. Cohen, "'Can Music Save Your Mortal Soul?': Assessing Scholarship Concerning the Rock-Religion Phenomenon," 2013, unpublished paper. My thanks to Jonathan for sharing this paper with me.

[21] Daniel Cavicchi, *Tramps Like Us: Music and Meaning among Springsteen Fans* (New York and Oxford: Oxford University Press, 1998); Linda K. Randall, *Finding Grace in the Concert Hall: Community and Meaning among Springsteen Fans* (Long Grove, IL: Waveland, 2011). Springsteen-based conversion narratives are not limited to his fans, as the following account from Clarence Clemons demonstrates: "Bruce is the greatest person I've ever met. He's the strongest person I've ever met. When I first met him it was like in the Bible where this guy met this guy and he says 'Lay down your thing and follow me,' and that's exactly the way I felt, man." Andrew Tyler, "Bruce Springsteen and the Wall of Faith," *New Musical Express*, November 15, 1975; reprinted in Burger, *Springsteen on Springsteen*, 43. It is worth noting that the word *fan* is an abbreviation of *fanatic*, whose religious overtones are already present in its Latin source: "related to the *fanum*, the temple," and thus "mad with divine inspiration."

speaking religious, touch on core spiritual concerns. Steve Turner writes that the "human problem, as Springsteen defines it in his work, is a basic lack of fulfillment. Surrounded by death, pain and fear, we human beings have to break our backs even to survive. Yet all the time we know, deep in our hearts, that we were created for greater things."[22] More recently, June Skinner Sawyers has characterized Springsteen as one of the most spiritual popular artists, in part because "[m]any of the characters in his songs are misfits and loners, losers and outcasts who feel out of place in the world ... They long for a kind of spiritual release but also for a reason to believe."[23]

The religious themes in Springsteen's lyrics are doubtless amplified by the famously revivalist mood of his concerts. Here is Robert Duncan's account of Springsteen's introduction to "Growing Up" at a concert in Houston. Springsteen explains that his parents had different career goals for him: his father wanted him to be a lawyer, and his mother wanted him to be an author. The family goes to the priest who refers them directly to God, whom Springsteen approaches reverentially but honestly, explaining that he only wants to play his guitar:

> He pauses again. The music swells slightly but otherwise, there's complete silence. The audience sits breathless, waiting to see: Can this Yankee rock 'n' roller conjure too? Springsteen resumes in a harsh, rushed whisper. "All of a sudden, there's this light in the sky above me and a great big voice booms out and says..." Beat. The music drops down. "Let it rock!"[24]

---

[22] Steve Turner, *Hungry for Heaven: Rock 'n' Roll and the Search for Redemption* (Downers Grove, IL: InterVarsity, 1995), 152-3.

[23] June Skinner Sawyers, "'Deliver Me from Nowhere': Spiritual Longing in the Music of Bruce Springsteen," paper presented at *Glory Days: A Bruce Springsteen Symposium, Sept. 9th-11th, 2005*, pages 1 and 4, respectively. See also Scott Wagar, "Life Right Now: Springsteen and Spirituality," in Kenneth Womack, Jerry Zolten, and Mark Bernhard, editors, *Bruce Springsteen, Cultural Studies, and the Runaway American Dream* (Burlington, VT: Ashgate, 2012), 163-74. A number of scholars have identified themes present in Springsteen's work and in biblical sources, without claiming that Springsteen is explicitly indebted to them. Thus, Jerry H. Gill, "The Gospel According to Bruce," *Theology Today* 45 (1988), 87-94, and Jacqueline E. Lapsley, "'Bring On Your Wrecking Ball': Psalm 73 and Public Witness," *Theology Today* 70 (2013), 62-68.

[24] Duncan, "Lawdamercy," 91.

In these monologues, rock itself becomes a pathway to a certain type of salvation. As Springsteen declared during the E Street Band's 2000 tour: "I can't promise you life everlasting, but I can promise you life *right now*."[25]

Given Springsteen's lyric themes and performance style, it is possible to situate him on the secular/sacred divide that has run through rock 'n' roll from its earliest days, and is plainly evident in many of the musicians Springsteen acknowledges as influences. For Elvis Presley, for example, rock 'n' roll was closely affiliated with country gospel: When Elvis, Jerry Lee Lewis, Carl Perkins, and Johnny Cash gathered for an impromptu jam session at Sun studios in 1956, they performed such songs as "Blessed Jesus Hold My Hand," "Keeper of the Key," and "Farther Along."[26] These gospel and country-gospel songs were the standards of the day, and the musical backdrop to many of the great early rock 'n' roll singers that Springsteen admired.[27] The same is true for the African-American Gospel tradition, the proving ground for so many R&B artists.[28] Indeed, many R&B songs were secularized versions of gospel works, including Ben E. King's "Stand by Me" (originally: "Stand by Me, Father"), Ray Charles "This Little Girl of Mine" (originally: "This Little Light of Mine"), and

---

[25] Bill Friskics-Warren, *I'll Take You There: Pop Music and the Urge for Transcendence* (New York: Continuum, 2005), 226. And see Larry David Smith's claim that Springsteen's shows are "a direct extension of the Southern black church and its long, joyous, liberating communal rituals," in *Bob Dylan, Bruce Springsteen, and American Song* (Westport, CT: Praeger, 2002), quoted in June Skinner Sawyers's introduction to *Racing in the Street: The Bruce Springsteen Reader*, 17.

[26] See Davin Seay with Mary Neely, *Stairway to Heaven: The Spiritual Roots of Rock 'n' Roll—From the King and Little Richard to Prince and Amy Grant* (New York: Ballantine, 1986); Joe Moscheo and Priscilla Beaulieu Presley, *The Gospel Side of Elvis* (New York: Center Street, 2007). On the Sun Studios jam session, see Seay and Neely, *Stairway to Heaven*, 50-51. The group came to be known as the "Million Dollar Quartet" and the recordings from that session were eventually released.

[27] Springsteen has said: "In the beginning, every musician has their genesis moment … Mine was 1956, Elvis on *The Ed Sullivan Show*. It was the evening I realized a white man could make magic, that you did not have to be constrained by your upbringing, by the way you looked, or by the social context," Keynote Speech at the 2012 *South by Southwest Music Festival*, in Burger, *Springsteen on Springsteen*, 388.

[28] See Teresa L. Reed, *The Holy Profane: Religion in Black Popular Music* (Lexington, KY: University of Kentucky Press, 2003); Jerma A. Jackson, *Singing in My Soul: Black Gospel Music in a Secular Age* (Chapel Hill: University of North Carolina Press, 2004).

the Dominoes "Have Mercy, Baby" (originally: "Have Mercy, Lord").[29] Springsteen's songs and performance might well be characterized as a secular version of religious songs and Pentecostal preaching.

This book takes a different tack, focusing on biblical and theological motifs in Springsteen's lyrics.[30] This approach is open to two interrelated objections. The first is that Springsteen is not a practicing Catholic and therefore could not be interested in biblical and theological material. Whether the premise of this objection is true or not, the conclusion is erroneous. We tend to think of theology as occurring within the confines of churches or seminaries, as learned discussions held by pious believers, when in truth many artists have engaged their religious traditions even though they do not identify as traditional adherents. The second objection is that many of Springsteen's songs are uncompromisingly this-worldly: girls and cars, love and loss. These songs, the objection goes, might deal with the human condition in some abstract sense, but not in an explicitly theological manner. What is lost in this claim is the way many modern

---

[29] See Reed, *Holy Profane*, 104. Examining the influence of Pentecostal musical traditions on the Isley Brothers' "Shout" (1959), with its call-and-response pattern and increased tempo leading up the crescendo on the word *shout*, Reed writes that the song "does more than mimic Pentecostalism; it *is* Pentecostalism!" (30). Springsteen's musical and cultural debt to R&B artists is well documented, not least by Springsteen himself. Even so, it is possible that the size of the debt remains underappreciated. Joel Dinerstein has argued that Springsteen "provided narratives for the deindustrialized dispossessed of the rust belt, and all have drawn upon African American musical models that straddle the sacred/secular crossroads," Joel Dinerstein, "The Soul Roots of Bruce Springsteen's American Dream," *American Music* 25 (2007), 468.

[30] A number of writers have addressed theological elements in Springsteen's writings, including Matthew Orel, "From Adam to Jesus: Springsteen's Use of Scripture," in Womack, Zolten, and Bernhard, *Bruce Springsteen, Cultural Studies, and the Runaway American Dream*, 145-162; Spencer L. Allen, "Mary Queen of Arkansas; Mary Queen of Heaven," paper presented at *Glory Days: A Bruce Springsteen Symposium, Sept. 9th-11th, 2005*; Stephen Hazan Arnoff, "A Covenant Reversed: Bruce Springsteen and the Promised Land," in Roxanne Harde and Irwin Streight, editors, *Reading the Boss: Interdisciplinary Approaches to the Works of Bruce Springsteen* (Lanham, MD; Lexington, 2010), 177-200; Paul Contino, "The Theology of St. Augustine and Bruce Springsteen: 'Everybody's Got a Hungry Heart'," and unpublished talk presented at Villanova University, October 29, 2009; Maria Diemling, "American Midrash: Biblical Motifs in the Work of Bruce Springsteen," in Lucie Dolezalová and Tamás Visi, editors, *Retelling the Bible: Literary, Historical, and Social Contexts* (Frankfurt/Main: Peter Lang, 2011), 355-368; Mark S. Graybill, "As Empty as Paradise": Reading Religion in Bruce Springsteen's *The Rising*," *Studies in American Culture* 33 (2010), 28-33; Jennifer Walter, "The Boss and the Bible: Biblical Imagery and the Spiritual Journey in the Songs of Bruce Springsteen," paper presented at *Glory Days: A Bruce Springsteen Symposium, Sept. 9th-11th, 2005*. Jeffrey Symynkywicz, *The Gospel According to Bruce Springsteen* (Louisville: Westminster John Knox, 2008) seeks to extract spiritual lessons from Springsteen's writings, a subtly but significantly different task than the one at hand.

writers—poets in particular—employ traditional themes in the service of non-traditional or even anti-traditional ends.[31]

One of the great scholars of Romanticism has characterized the movement in its entirety as an artistic return "to the stark drama and suprarational mysteries of the Christian story,"[32] though not a return to traditional Christian beliefs and practices. Percy Bysshe Shelley wrote in unabashedly religious terms that "a poet participates in the eternal, the infinite, and the one" and that "poetry is indeed something divine,"[33] even while adhering to the claims of his earlier book, *The Necessity of Atheism*.[34] Or consider William Wordsworth's verse:

> Of Genius, Power
> Creation, and Divinity itself,
> I have been speaking.
> Not of outward things
> Done visibly for other minds—words, signs,
> Symbols or actions—but of my own heart
> Have I been speaking.
> (1805 *Prelude* 3.171-77)[35]

Wordsworth states unequivocally that "of . . . Divinity itself/I have been speaking" but immediately clarifies that he is not referring to the traditional notion of a transcendent God, but rather "of my own heart/Have I been speaking." The divine *is* Wordsworth's own heart, his own inner being, for his poetry does not treat of "outward things," that is, "words, signs/

---

[31] Much of the remainder of the chapter addresses the relationship between religious sources and modern poets and songwriters. I return to Springsteen only at the end of the chapter.

[32] M. H. Abrams, *Natural Supernaturalism: Tradition and Revolution in Romantic Literature* (New York: Norton, 1971), 66; and see the more recent work of Ian Balfour, *The Rhetoric of Romantic Prophecy* (Stanford: Stanford University Press, 2002).

[33] Percy Bysshe Shelley, "A Defence of Poetry," in Donald H. Reiman and Neil Fraistat, editors, *Shelley's Poetry and Prose* (New York: Norton, 2002), 513 and 531, respectively.

[34] *The Necessity of Atheism* was co-authored with Thomas Jefferson Hogg. Shelley was vociferously critical of the church throughout his life.

[35] See Geoffrey Hartman, "'*Was it for this . . .?* Wordsworth and the Birth of the Gods," in Kenneth R. Johnston, Gilbert Chaitin, et al., editors, *Romantic Revolutions: Criticism and Theory* (Bloomington and Indianapolis: Indiana University Press, 1990), 8-25.

symbols or actions." Wordsworth, then, is concerned with the divine, but not with any of the external rituals or institutions of traditional religion. Now, can the sentiment expressed in these lines be classified as religious? In one sense, the answer must be affirmative, as Wordsworth considers "Divinity itself"—and surely this is a religious undertaking. But in another sense, Wordsworth's negation of the external manifestations of religion—more bluntly, of the church—might well be taken as anti-religious.

The situation is fundamentally similar for the American Romantic tradition, exemplified in Walt Whitman's transfer of the crown of prophecy to the poet:

> The prophet and the bard,
> Shall yet maintain themselves, in higher stages yet,
> Shall mediate to the Modern, to Democracy, interpret yet to them,
> God and eidólons.[36]

In Whitman's lexicon, *eidolon* refers to a visible manifestation of the divine, so he is assigning to the poet ("the bard") a role as elevated as that of the prophet—to communicate and interpret the divine to humankind. Do these lines express a religious sentiment? Whitman has elevated the poet to the level of prophet, arguably an expansion of the religious realm into the earthly; yet one could claim with equal force that the divine has been lowered into the human realm, that the prophet, in other words, has been secularized.[37]

This non-traditional, revisionary poetic engagement with religious themes continues today.[38] Let me cite, by way of illustration, two

---

[36] "Eidólons" in Walt Whitman, *The Complete Works of Walt Whitman* (Wordsworth Poetry Library; Hertfordshire, UK: 1995), 6-8.

[37] On Whitman as a religious author see David Kuebrich, "Religion and the Poet-Prophet," in Donald D. Kummings, editor, *A Companion to Walt Whitman* (Hoboken, NJ: Wiley, 2009), 197-215, and, more fully, idem, *Minor Prophecy: Walt Whitman's New American Religion* (Bloomington: Indiana University Press, 1989).

[38] See Chana Kronfeld's discussion in *On the Margins of Modernism: Decentering Literary History* (Berkeley and Los Angeles: University of California Press, 1996), especially chapter five, "Theories of Allusion and Imagist Intertextuality: When Iconoclasts Evoke the Bible"; the same dynamic permeates Kronfeld's more recent study, *The Full Severity of Compassion: The Poetry of Yehuda Amichai* (Stanford: Stanford University Press, 2016).

twentieth-century poems that exemplify some of the ways modern authors engage traditional theological motifs. Czeslaw Milosz's "An Honest Description of Myself with a Glass of Whiskey at An Airport, Let Us Say, in Minneapolis,"[39] begins with a description of the speaker's failing senses and the resulting difficulty he experiences hearing and seeing women. The poem first responds to this loss by affirming the speaker's sexual desire—"I see their legs in miniskirts, slacks, wavy fabrics/Peep at each one separately, at their buttocks and thighs, lulled by the imaginings of porn." But these carnal yearnings are soon shown to be manifestations of a broader erotic impulse: "It's not that I desire these creatures precisely; I desire everything, and they are like a sign of ecstatic union." Traditionally, the phrase "ecstatic union" refers to a mystical encounter with God, facilitated by prayer or mystical experience, while the lascivious description of the women in the opening lines of the poem suggests a more carnal form of ecstatic union. Ultimately, neither interpretation can carry the day: the traditional sense of "ecstatic union" is inadequate because Milosz does not introduce a divine partner for the union; the sexual, because the poem states that women are *not* merely objects of sexual desire, but rather markers of a much fundamental, metaphysical yearning. The ecstatic union, then, is neither religious in any traditional sense, nor earthly—if by *earthly* we mean bereft of spiritual meaning. The un-decidable suspension between a heavenly and earthly poetic is confirmed in the poem's conclusion:

> If I should accede one day to Heaven, it must be there as it is here, except that I
> will be rid of my dull senses and my heavy bones.
> Changed into pure seeing, I will absorb, as before, the proportions of human bodies, the color of irises, a Paris street in June at dawn, all of it incomprehensible, incomprehensible the multitude of visible things.

---

[39] *New York Review of Books* 12/20/2001, translated from the Polish by Robert Hass and Czeslaw Milosz.

Again we encounter a religious term, *heaven*, whose traditional meaning—the transcendent realm, opposed to the earthly—is reworked. For in the poem's heaven "it must be there as it is here," meaning that the dichotomy between the heavenly and earthly is undermined. Though the poet imagines being freed of the burden of his corporeality, he does not become an incorporeal spirit, but rather embraces a higher form of sensing, "pure seeing." Thus transformed, he will be able to fully appreciate the same sights that moved him in life—human beauty, nature, the majesty of a Paris dawn—only in a more direct and unmediated manner.

Milosz, then, uses religious terminology to forge a series of intermediary spaces between the traditional dichotomies of heaven and earth, the spirit and the flesh. Women are at once the carnal objects of pornographic fantasies, and manifestations of a metaphysical yearning; heaven is "as it is here," but unencumbered by the weight of the body; the afterlife is a site of purity, but a sensory purity of refined vision. The poem, in other words, creates a realm of immanent transcendence.[40]

Like Milosz's "An Honest Description," Grace Paley's poem "Psalm" employs traditional religious terminology in new ways, albeit to a different effect.

> their shoes are stuccoed with sawdust and blood
> the two young butchers walk singing together on ninth avenue
> the sun is out because it is the lunch hour
> they kick the melting snow and splash into deep puddles
> then they embrace one another in the cold air
> for water and singing may wash away the blood of the lamb[41]

The poem's title, "Psalm," posits a continuity with a biblical genre largely devoted to the praise of God,[42] but its content offers a distinctly

---

[40] In later works, Milosz laments the loss of the traditional division of this world and the next. In the title poem of the collection *Second Space* he asks: "Have we really lost faith in that other space?/Have they vanished forever, both Heaven and Hell? ... Let us implore that it be returned to us/That second space," Czeslaw Milosz, *Second Space: New Poems*, translated by Robert Haas (New York: Ecco, 2005), 3.

[41] Grace Paley, *Begin Again: Collected Poems* (New York: Farrar, Straus, Giroux, 2001), 19.

[42] Praise of God but also, as Ben Sommer notes, aggrieved complaints to God.

unbiblical sketch of two young New York butchers on lunch break. The young men are close friends, passing their lunch hour in shared song and playful walks through the streets of Manhattan's lower west side (hearkening back to a time when New York's Meatpacking District was home to a meatpacking industry), warmly hugging before, one assumes, returning to their respective stations. Nothing about this exchange explains why Paley titled the poem "Psalm". It is not until the final words of the poem that the reader encounters an unambiguous religious reference: "for water and singing may wash away the blood of the lamb."

The phrase "the blood of the lamb" is a standard reference to Jesus' blood based on the words John the Baptist utters upon seeing Jesus for the first time—"Here is the Lamb of God who takes away the sin of the world" (John 1:29).[43] To contemporary readers, this may appear a perplexing moniker: why would John identify Christ with a lamb, and how is that identification tied to removing the sin of the world? In the uniformly Jewish religious world of Jesus and his earliest followers, however, the reference to the lamb was readily identified with the lamb that was offered as part of the Jerusalem Temple's Passover sacrifice—the holiday during which Jesus died. Paul speaks of Jesus' death in precisely these terms: "For our Paschal lamb, Christ, has been sacrificed" (1 Corinthians 5:7). The Paschal lamb of the temple, in turn, is a reminder of the lamb slaughtered by the Israelites in Egypt on the night of the Exodus, its blood smeared on the Israelite doorposts to protect their children from the final plague, the death of the firstborn. Whatever the original intent of John's words,[44] once the Gospel of John referred to Jesus

---

[43] The title "Lamb of God" appears again at John 1:36. Unless otherwise noted, all Bible quotes are from the NRSV.

[44] Scholars debate why John speaks of the sacrificial lamb in terms of atonement, when the Passover sacrifice is not so characterized in the Hebrew Bible. According to some, the lamb is an oblique reference to the sacrificial goats that the High Priest offered during the Yom Kippur (Day of Atonement) ritual and that are explicitly described as washing away sin. According to others, though not presented in these terms in the Hebrew Bible, by the time of John the Baptist, the Passover sacrifice had come to be associated with the forgiveness of sins. On the representation of Jesus' death as analogous to the Paschal offering see Jeffrey Siker, "Yom Kippuring Passover: Recombinant Sacrifice in Early Christianity," in *Ritual and Metaphor: Sacrifice in the Bible*, Christian A. Eberhart, editor, (Atlanta: Society of Biblical Literature Press, 2011), 65-82. My thanks to Mira Balberg for this reference.

as the Lamb of God "who takes away the sin of the world," the blood of the lamb was understood as a powerful symbolic substance. Thus, in the Book of Revelation, the blood of the lamb is an element in the victory of the archangel Michael and the hosts of heaven over Satan (who appears as a dragon): "And war broke out in heaven; Michael and his angels fought against the dragon... [and] conquered him by the blood of the Lamb and by the word of their testimony" (Revelation 12:7-11).

In Grace Paley's poem, the phrase "blood of the lamb" no longer refers to a metaphysical entity, but to the physical blood of the lambs slaughtered in New York's meatpacking district. And rather than wash away sin, the blood of the lamb is itself washed off by "water and singing," a phrase that embodies the this-worldly orientation of a poem about two young men and the lunch break they spend together laughing and walking through puddles. Paley's "Psalm" is not composed for the greater glory of God, but for the greater glory of man—the everyday joy of shared friendship and laughter. Indeed, Paley repeatedly indicates that the two butchers are graced, e.g., when she refers to their grimy shoes as "*stuccoed* with sawdust and blood." She also transforms in a subtle but poetically powerful manner the Psalter's well-known claim that "the heavens are telling the glory of God" (Psalm 19:1). In the world of the poem, the sun shines "*because* it is the lunch hour"—emerging for the sake of the young laborers. And note Paley's interesting statement that the blood of the lamb is washed away by water and *singing*, which is clearly not true of physical blood. What might be washed away is the accreted layers of religious symbolism: the joyous song of friends on lunch break washes away the metaphysics of sin and sacrifice associated with the blood of the lamb.

Much more could be said about Paley's poem, but for the present argument I want to focus on the points of commonality between Milosz and Paley, and the points of difference. The two share a poetic sensibility that mobilizes traditional religious terms in non-traditional ways. Milosz's ecstatic union is not that of the Christian mystical tradition, though it does draw on it, nor his heaven the heaven of Christian theology; Paley's psalm celebrates man, not God, and the blood of the lamb is stripped of its theological force. But the poets offer different visions: Milosz forges an intermediary space that partakes in traditional transcendence even while it remains rooted in the material world, while Paley celebrates a fully immanent reality, cheerfully discarding hoary metaphysical categories.

Though on the whole more concerned with this-worldly themes, a similar engagement with traditional sources can be identified in popular music as well. In "Jesus Christ," Woody Guthrie writes of Jesus coming to twentieth-century America and being killed for preaching his gospel of economic justice.[45] Jesus instructs the rich and powerful, specifically various officials (including the priest) to sell their luxury belongings and give the money to the poor. But Jesus' entreaties do not sway the rich and powerful, quite the contrary: upset by the message he is preaching, they "laid Jesus Christ in His grave." In the final stanza, Guthrie shifts to his present day:

> This song was written in New York City
> Of rich man, preacher, and slave
> If Jesus was to preach what He preached in Galilee,
> They would lay poor Jesus in His grave.

Is Guthrie's song true to the Gospel? Guthrie has distilled a single aspect of Jesus' teaching, care for the poor, and made it the focus of the song. And this is, to be sure, an element of Jesus' message:

> Then Jesus said to his disciples, "Truly I tell you, it will be hard for a rich person to enter the kingdom of heaven. Again I tell you, it is easier for a camel to go through the eye of a needle than for someone who is rich to enter the kingdom of God." (Matthew 19:23-24)

Woody Guthrie's message is, then, rooted in the teachings of Jesus: had Jesus arrived at New York in 1940 and exhorted people to renounce their personal property (a position closely associated with Communism),

---

[45] See James Knight, "'I Ain't Got No Home in This World Anymore': Protest and Promise in Woody Guthrie and the Jesus Tradition," in Gilmour, *Call Me the Seeker*, 17-33.

he might have met with the same fate as in first century Roman Palestine. But Guthrie's exclusive focus on economic inequality omits key elements of the Gospels, including the Virgin Birth, Jesus' miracles, the teachings of the imminent Kingdom of God, and any Christological doctrine regarding Jesus' status. Woody Guthrie's Jesus is a person deeply committed to social justice—no less and no more. In this sense, the song both mobilizes and revises the teachings of the New Testament.

Or consider Bob Dylan's reworking of Genesis 22, the story of the Binding of Isaac, in "Highway 61 Revisited." In the biblical account, God makes a covenant with Abraham, promising that Abraham will sire a son and God "will make of you a great nation, and I will bless you, and make your name great so that you will be a blessing" (Genesis 12:2). Miraculously, Abraham's aged wife, Sarah, becomes pregnant and bears a son, Isaac, through whom God's promise will be fulfilled. And yet, years later, when God commands Abraham to slaughter his own son as an offering, Abraham sets off unquestioningly to fulfill God's instruction. [God] said, 'Take your son, your only son Isaac, whom you love, and go to the land of Moriah, and offer him there as a burnt offering' … So Abraham rose early in the morning, saddled his donkey, and took two of his young men with him, and his son Isaac (Genesis 22:2-3).

The entire sequence spans two verses—God commands, and Abraham obeys without protest. In "Highway 61, Revisited," Dylan imagines a very different exchange between God and Abraham:

> Oh God said to Abraham, "Kill me a son"
> Abe says, "Man, you must be puttin' me on"
> God say, "No." Abe say, "What?"
> God say, "You can do what you want Abe, but
> The next time you see me comin' you better run"
> Well Abe says, "Where do you want this killin' done?"
> God says. "Out on Highway 61"[46]

[46] Bob Dylan, *Highway 61, Revisited* (Columbia, 1965).

As numerous commentators have noted, Dylan transforms the biblical narrative in a number of ways: the irreverent reference to Abraham as *Abe*, the address of God as *Man*, God's bullying response to Abraham's incredulity, and Abraham's subsequent acquiescence (he asks *where?* and not *why?*).[47] Like Woody Guthrie and (despite the obvious difference in tenor) the poets surveyed above, "Highway 61 Revisited" is firmly located outside the realm of traditional religious discourse, though much of the song's poetic power is rooted in its revisionist account of this well-known biblical episode.

I have not given any of the works surveyed here their proper due, but my intent has not been to discuss these writers for their own sake, but rather to bring to the fore the tradition of poets and songwriters that draw on the linguistic and symbolic reserves of religious sources as a way of transforming traditional doctrines.[48] Much of the analysis that follows is dedicated to the proposition that a significant portion of Springsteen's work ought be read as theologically inflected poetry, irrespective his personal piety or impiety.

---

[47] See the discussion in Neil Corcoran, "Death's Honesty," in Neil Corcoran, editor, *"Do You, Mr. Jones?" Bob Dylan with the Poets and the Professors* (London: Chatto and Windus, 2002), 143-74. Note also James Goodman's comment that "Dylan's Abraham is, briefly, a sixties rebel, but note that neither the angel of God nor any other form of deliverance is on its way. Sacrifice becomes killing in a setting that is less Genesis than the end of days," James Goodman, *But Where is the Lamb? Imagining the Story of Abraham and Isaac* (New York: Schocken, 2013), 208. My thanks to James Goodman for sharing his work with me.

[48] The dichotomy between traditional and non-traditional is, in significant ways, illusory. The claims of traditionalists notwithstanding, traditions are never truly static; they are forever adapting to new historical circumstance. The division between tradition, on the one hand, and the innovative appropriation of traditional themes, on the other, is not, then, categorical. Nonetheless, the traditional/non-traditional distinction is meaningful as a reflection of the (self-) understanding of the individuals employing the religious motifs. For example, even though the doctrine of papal infallibility was not formally accepted as Catholic dogma until the relatively late date of 1870, most Catholics consider it part of their religious tradition, and a writer opposed to the doctrine might well understand himself and be understood by others as anti-traditional. In the same way, the claim implicit in Springsteen's song title "Jesus Was an Only Son" does not cohere with the New Testament testimonies regarding James, the brother of the Lord (Paul writes: "Then after three years I did go up to Jerusalem to visit Cephas and stayed with him for fifteen days; but I did not see any other apostle except James the Lord's brother" [Galatians 1:18-19]). Nonetheless, I consider the phrase (though not the song) traditional because it expresses what has come to be understood as the traditional view. Traditional status, in other words, refers to how a claim is perceived, rather than to its historical truth. I thank Gayle Lasater Pagnoni for pushing me to clarify this point.

Of course, Bruce Springsteen does not identify as a poet, and some readers may wonder whether the literary approach I am advocating is suited for a man of his background. A response couched in biographical terms would point out that, for much of his early career, Springsteen wrote in a style that was knowingly poetic and sustained the "new Dylan" moniker that first accompanied and then plagued him.[49] Moreover, Springsteen's interviews are studded with references to literary and cinematic influences, as when Springsteen tells Will Percy about his deep engagement with the work of Catholic author and essayist Walker Percy (the interviewer's uncle), and speaks of his literary influences more broadly: "[t]he really important reading that I did began in my late twenties, with authors like Flannery O'Connor," followed by quotes from Walt Whitman and William Carlos Williams, among others.[50] It is, then, at the very least, plausible to read Springsteen as a more literary writer than is often assumed. A more powerful support for the approach I adopt is that close, theologically attuned, readings of Springsteen's lyrics yield meaningful insights into his artistry. How these insights are to be squared with his public image is a secondary concern.

The relatively narrow thematic focus of the book means I analyze the lyrics of a limited set of songs, rather than attempting an overview of Springsteen's entire corpus. As a consequence, I include some relatively obscure songs but omit some of Springsteen's most famous works—including entire albums, e.g., *The Wild, the Innocent & the E Street Shuffle*

---

[49] The comparison between Springsteen and Dylan was so cliché by 1973 that Steve Turner wrote an article titled "Was Bob Dylan the Previous Bruce Springsteen?" (*New Musical Express*, October 6, 1973; reprinted in Burger, *Springsteen on Springsteen*, 8-12).

[50] The interview appeared in the Spring 1998 issue of *DoubleTake*; reprinted in Phillips and Masur, *Talk About a Dream*, 218-32 ("The really important reading," "Walt Whitman," and "William Carlos Williams" are found in Philips and Masur, *Talk About a Dream*, 220, 224, and 225, respectively). See also the wonderful statement in Springsteen 2003 interview with Ken Tucker: "I tell ya, those three [recent] books by Philip Roth—*American Pastoral*, *I Married a Communist*, *The Human Stain*—just knocked me on my ass. To be [in one's 60s] making work that strong and so full of revelations about love and emotional pain—man, that's the way to live your artistic life: Sustain, sustain, sustain," *Entertainment Weekly*, February 28, 2003; reprinted in Phillips and Masur, *Talk About a Dream*, 279. Note the peaceful coexistence of Springsteen's blue-collar and intellectual personas, as his colloquial language ("I'll tell ya ... [they] knocked me on my ass") expresses enthusiasm for Philip Roth's ability to create literature that is strong and emotionally revelatory.

and *Born in the U.S.A.*, neither of which contains many biblical references. The book's scope is further curtailed in that it examines Springsteen's lyrics in isolation from his music. This admittedly artificial division is due in part to the fact that my scholarly training lies in textual, not musical, analysis. But even casual statements about a song's music should be approached with caution when it comes to Springsteen, as the relationship between the lyrics and the music is often less straightforward than it appears. We find, for example, an obvious tension between the driving, anthem-like sound of "Born in the U.S.A." (*Born in the U.S.A.*) and the song's somber lyrics, that chronicle the mistreatment of Vietnam veterans after the war.[51] Or consider his statement that "Ramrod" (*The River*), a raunchy, hard-rocking celebration of the car-as-woman (and vice versa) is "one of the saddest songs I've ever written."[52] In any case, my approach is intended as a complement to other disciplinary frameworks that provide a deeper understanding of Springsteen's work (class, gender, politics, race, and more).

As I will argue in what follows, Springsteen's writing up to *Darkness on the Edge of Town* follows a fairly clear trajectory: one set of songs critiques traditional religious doctrines and institutions, another holds out the possibility of an immanent, this-worldly salvation. *Darkness on the Edge of Town* turns away from these earlier themes, dismantling the theological possibilities delineated in the earlier albums, and endorsing in their stead a darker vision, one that draws its core elements from the apocalyptic tradition. The book's first part, "Early Works," examines this trajectory. After *Darkness on the Edge of Town* (and a limited number of songs from *The River*), it becomes difficult to analyze Springsteen's work chronologically, and so the book's second part explores the motifs of "Sin," "Grace and Redemption," and "The Struggle Within." Part three, "Springsteen's Midrash," examines songs that reinterpret biblical narratives: "Swallowed Up (In the Belly of the Whale)" on the Book of Jonah; "Into the Fire" on the death of the prophet Elijah; "Adam Raised a Cain" on Cain and Abel; and "Jesus Was an Only Son," on the Passion narrative.

---

[51] The more somber version of "Born in the U.S.A." released on *Tracks* (and originally recorded for *Nebraska*) is a better "fit" for the lyrics, but it is not the one that Springsteen included on the album.

[52] Cited in Rob Kirkpatrick, *Magic in the Night: The Words and Music of Brice Springsteen* (New York: St. Martin's, 2009), 95.

Early Works

CHAPTER ONE

The Sacred Profaned

Much of the academic discussion of Springsteen and religion involves two related errors. Many studies draw on a very small sample of Springsteen's writings yet claim to have uncovered his one view on a given topic; others survey a larger set of songs but labor under the assumption that his views have remained static, so that the insights gleaned from one album (usually *Born to Run*) can be extended to later works. An example of the former is Greeley's coronation of Springsteen as a "Catholic minstrel" (discussed in the introduction), which is based on *Tunnel of Love* alone, ignoring the albums that precede and follow;[1] of the latter, George Yamin examines several of Springsteen's early albums, but does so in a way that glosses over the theological differences between the songs: "[The] most obvious evidence for a religious element in his

[1] Greely claims that the release of *Tunnel of Love* "may be a more important Catholic event in this country than the visit of Pope John Paul II" ("The Catholic Imagination of Bruce Springsteen," 236). As Ben Sommer notes (personal communication), the album is widely regarded as dealing with Springsteen's divorce, so it is ironic that Greeley would characterize it as such an affirmative statement of Catholic theology.

music may be found in the titles of many Springsteen songs. For example, allusions to the Old Testament are present in such songs as 'Adam Raised a Cain,' 'Lost in the Flood,' and 'The Promised Land.' In addition, there are frequent references to religious terminology, in such titles as 'The Angel,' 'Spirit in the Night,' and 'It's Hard to Be a Saint in the City.'"[2] Yamin's groupings indicate a superficial thematic commonality among songs that contain "religious elements," but fail to account for the disparate, even antithetical theological positions these songs stake out (see below). In an attempt to avoid these pitfalls, the present chapter examines a number of songs from Springsteen's early period that contain biblical and theological elements and express a relatively coherent perspective—rebellious and sometimes harshly anti-religious.[3]

One of the earliest biblical references in Springsteen's writing is found in a touching request for guidance in a song that was never recorded:

> Jesus, Mary, and Joseph
> Can you help a lost sheep please
> Won't you show me the way
> Cause I got more confused each day and
> I got calluses on my knees[4]

The tone is not antagonistic, but the singer is plainly distressed by his deepening confusion and lack of response from Jesus, Joseph, and Mary; the reference to calluses on his knees suggests the singer is growing impatient. Others songs are more openly rebellious. The unreleased Steel Mill song "Sister Theresa" is an adolescent love song (lust song?) to a nun, who "needs a man to love."[5] Of course, Sister

---

[2] George Y. Yamin, Jr. "The Theology of Bruce Springsteen," *Journal of Religious Studies* 16 (1990), 4.

[3] These albums also contain a second, more constructive theological perspective, one that I address in the next chapter.

[4] The song (or song fragment) appears in one of Springsteen's song notebooks from 1968 (http://www.springsteenlyrics.com/lyrics.php?song=jesusmaryandjoseph; retrieved, 1/13/2016).

[5] Steel Mill is an early Springsteen band that performed from the end of 1969 to the beginning of 1971. The lyrics to "Sister Theresa," which was first played in 1970, are available here: http://www.springsteenlyrics.com/lyrics.php?song=sistertheresa (retrieved 3/15/2016).

Theresa claims she already has one—"you say you're married to Jesus Christ, and that he's in your bedroom every night." But Jesus' (physical) absence leads the singer to irreverently wonder "why's he treat you so cruel? Is he jealous, or just a fool?" The singer's promise that he can make Sister Theresa "smile" is a bit of youthful sexual bravado, that is also a pointed reversal of the Church's traditional priority of the Spirit over the Flesh. While Sister Theresa devotes her life to the former, the singer champions the latter. Rebellion of a different form is evident in Springsteen's "Where Was Jesus in Ohio?" another song from his early days with Steel Mill.[6] Written in the wake of the Kent State shootings in May, 1970 the song asks the poignant rhetorical question: "Will the sun ever shine again, will the moon ever smile again ... And where was Jesus in Ohio?" This question carries an implicit critique: what good are the Church's teachings if they cannot prevent brutal miscarriages of justice? But the full force of Springsteen's rebellion does not become evident until *Greetings from Asbury Park, N.J.*

"It's Hard to Be a Saint in the City"
(Greetings from Asbury Park, N.J.)

"It's Hard to Be a Saint in the City" opens with a first-person account of a young man, something of a dandy, who likens himself to a bursting supernova, strutting like Brando and dancing like Casanova in a smooth jacket and his slicked-back hair. As the song progresses, it becomes clear that the singer is mixed up in some shady business whose precise nature is never made clear: he is the "king of the alley," "the pimp's main prophet," "a backstreet gambler" who wields a blackjack. So even as the refrain laments that it is hard to be a saint in the city, the singer gives every indication he relishes his unsaintly status. Walking through his neighborhood, he notes with pride how "the sisters fell back and said 'Don't that man look pretty'," and he ignores a corner cripple crying out for aid.

[6] There is only one known performance of "Where Was Jesus in Ohio?" On either June 19 or 20, 1970, a little over a month after the Kent State shootings, Springsteen performed the song at a Steel Mill concert in Richmond, Virginia, see http://www.springsteenlyrics.com/lyrics/w/wherewasjesusinohio.php (retrieved 10/13/2015).

The scene shifts abruptly as, in the middle of his stroll, the singer is tempted by the devil: "The devil appeared like Jesus through the steam in the street, showin' me a hand I knew even the cops couldn't beat." The diabolical temptation recalls Jesus' desert encounter with and threefold temptation by the Devil: "Then Jesus was led up by the Spirit into the wilderness to be tempted by the devil" (Matthew 4:1). The Devil first tempts Jesus by asking him to display his powers by turning stones into loaves of bread to sate his hunger; then the Devil suggests that Jesus hurl himself off the pinnacle of the Temple to force God to save him; when these fail, the Devil offers Jesus all the riches in the world if only he worship him. Jesus counters each temptation with a scriptural verse that refutes the Devil's claim.[7] The singer in "It's Hard to Be a Saint in the City" is not versed in Scripture, so rather than confront the devil's temptation through holy writ, he flees, diving down to the tunnels of the subway. Alas, he is out of the frying pan and, literally, into the fire, since in Springsteen's poetic transformation, the New York subway has become hell itself. This was already suggested when the Devil appeared "through the steam in the street," the mist billowing through the subway grids into the cold New York air likened to smoke rising from a subterranean inferno. So it is no surprise that when the singer enters the subway, finds himself surrounded by passengers who "sit just like the living dead," and he begins to realize that "it's too hot in these tunnels, you can get hit up by the heat." He rises to leave, but the dead push him back into his seat in an attempt to trap him in the infernal realm they inhabit. He feels his heart racing as he struggles to regain his footing, until finally he manages to get "out of that hole" and return to the street.[8]

Is the singer a modern-day Jesus? Though the shared temptation scene might suggest such an interpretation, the song contains a number of indications to the contrary. Consider the people the singer sees on the city jaunt described in the first stanza—the sisters who say "Don't that man look pretty?" as he passes. I do not want to press this point (more of

---

[7] The Scripture in question, Jesus' Scripture, is the Hebrew Bible, also known as the Old Testament. For a detailed discussion of Jesus' use of the Hebrew Bible in his responses to the devil, see Dale C. Allison, Jr., *The Intertextual Jesus: Scripture in Q* (Harrisburg, PA: Trinity, 2000), 25-29.

[8] Note the phonetic assonance between *hole* and *hell.*

a suggestion, really), but since the song alludes to the Gospel narrative of Christ's temptation, it is worth noting that *sisters* can refer to nuns, as we find in a number of Springsteen's early songs including "Sister Theresa," "Resurrection," and "Living Rock 'n' Roll."[9] If the women admiring our singer belong to a religious order, and his mere presence elicits in them potentially lustful admiration, he is even less of a saint: though the singer escapes the Devil's temptation, he himself is a tempter.

The religious reading of *sisters* finds additional support in the event that follows: "the cripple on the corner cried out 'Nickels for your pity'." To this point, the song has focused on the singer's looks, clothing, swagger, and so on. Why does Springsteen introduce an alms-begging cripple into this scene? Because his presence underlines the contrast between Jesus' saintliness and the singer's lack of compassion. Jesus regularly heals cripples, for instance when scribes questioned his authority to forgive sins, Jesus turned to a paralytic he said: "'I say to you, stand up, take your mat and go home.' And he stood up, and immediately took the mat and went out before all of them" (Mark 2:11-12).[10] The singer in "It's Hard to Be a Saint in the City," in contrast, does not heal the cripple; in fact, he does not give him alms or so much as acknowledge his cries for help. The singer's behavior marks him as a morally perverted version of Jesus.

Does the temptation scene transform the singer? Alas, no. The most striking indication that the singer is being contrasted rather than likened to Jesus occurs after his ascent from the subway/inferno. He has overcome the Devil's temptation, but what of it? When Jesus triumphs, "the devil left him, and suddenly angels came and waited on him" (Matthew 4:11). Despite what should be a transformative encounter with the Devil and

---

[9] "Sister Theresa" was discussed above, "Resurrection" is discussed in the following chapter, and "Living Rock 'n' Roll" in chapter five.

[10] See similar healing narratives in Matthew 8 (Peter's mother-in-law), Matthew 9 (healing the blind), Matthew 12, Matthew 14 (Jesus heals the multitude). When Jesus sends his disciples out into the world, he commissions them to "cure the sick" (Matthew 10:8). Though not one of the commissioned disciples, Paul too cures cripples: "In Lystra there was a man sitting who could not use his feet and had never walked, for he had been crippled from birth. He listened to Paul as he was speaking. And Paul, looking at him intently and seeing that he had faith to be healed, said in a loud voice, 'Stand upright on your feet.' And the man sprang up and began to walk" (Acts 14:8-10).

a harrowing escape from hell, the singer repeats the line he sang before entering the subway and continues his strut through the familiar urban landscape, very much the same man. The Devil's temptation has had no real effect on him, and his continued lament that "it's so hard to be a saint in the city" emphasizes just how desperately the singer is rooted in the profane. He has overcome the Devil's temptation, but emerged no closer to sainthood—or even to the core human empathy necessary for giving alms to a cripple beggar. The song thus inverts the Gospel narrative: the Jesus figure turns out to be an inveterate hood, the moment of potential salvation comes to naught, and we find ourselves at the end of the song precisely where we started—forced to recognize that it *is* hard to be a saint in the city.

"Lost in the Flood" ***(Greetings from Asbury Park, N.J.)***

"Lost in the Flood" is a triptych of thematically related scenes, each depicting a different aspect of a morally corrupt American landscape through starkly reworked biblical imagery. The first portrays a soldier, a "gunner," back from war abroad (presumably Vietnam, given the timeframe of Springsteen's writing) confronting an American landscape as foreign and threatening as any battlefield.

> They're breakin' beams and crosses with a spastic's reelin'
> perfection
> Nuns run bald through Vatican halls, pregnant, pleadin'
> Immaculate Conception
> And everybody's wrecked on Main Street from drinking
> unholy blood

The anti-religious animus of the scene is obvious in the depiction of the pregnant nuns. The Gospel account emphatically distances Mary's pregnancy from sexual intercourse, asserting that she was "found to be with child from the Holy Spirit" (Matthew 1:18), a point the angel reiterates to Joseph, Mary's fiancé, telling him: "do not be afraid to take Mary as your wife, for the child conceived in her is from the Holy Spirit" (Matthew 1:20). The church, and Catholicism in particular, took Mary's virginity as an aspirational model for women, and a requirement for those who commit themselves to the church. But in the Gunner's world, pregnant nuns are overrunning the Vatican, physical proof that these women failed to uphold their vows of chastity, and perhaps an indication that supposedly celibate priests share the blame,[11] all in the putative center of Catholic piety. In addition to their carnal sin, the nuns are "pleading Immaculate Conception," refusing, that is, to admit their transgression, and instead invoking Mary's precedent in an attempt to absolve themselves.[12] Moreover, their attempt at self-exoneration is itself a theological transgression, as it plays into a long-standing anti-Christian polemical claim that the Virgin Birth was fabricated by Mary to conceal her sexual impropriety.

The stanza's third line presses the theological critique. In the course of the Last Supper, after predicting his betrayal, Jesus turned to his disciples, blessed a loaf of bread and said "take, eat; this is my body" (Matthew 26:26), then gave them wine, saying "this is my blood" (Matthew 26:28). On the basis of these statements, the Eucharist—the ritual of drinking sacramental wine and taking communion bread—developed. But where Christ's blood offers salvation, in the Gunner's town "everybody's wrecked on Main Street from drinking unholy blood." The image reverses both biblical and Norman Rockwell ideals. The town has a Main Street and, in keeping with idealized depictions of small-town America, all its residents are gathered there for a shared activity, but one that is decidedly unwholesome: imbibing unholy blood. Where Christ's blood saves, the town's leads to debauchery, as unnamed individuals are "breaking beams and crosses with a spastic reeling perfection" in an anti-Christian frenzy. The stanza ends when the Gunner walks toward what appears to be mud, and, despite the singer's calling out "that's quicksand, that ain't mud," continues walking until he is lost in the flood.

[11] This point was made to me by John Rak (personal communication).

[12] "Immaculate Conception" is the Catholic doctrine that Mary, though conceived biologically, was free of the stain of original sin. However, the phrase is often confused with the doctrine of Jesus' Virgin Birth, as it appears to be here.

The second scene tells of a weekend stock car driver named Jimmy, who passes his time telling racing stories. The song does not indicate his concern for otherworldly matters or any commitment to the spiritual, but in the religiously confused world of "Lost in the Flood," that does not dissuade the kids from calling him "Jimmy the Saint." The narrative that unfolds hinges on the ironic contrast between Jimmy's stated and actual fates. An inscription on the side of his motorcycle proclaims him "Bound for Glory," a phrase that alludes to the theological concept of glory and to the well-known gospel song about a train that is "bound for glory, don't carry nothing but the righteous and the holy."[13] Jimmy's assertion that he is "bound for glory" identifies him as one of the chosen who will be granted God's glory. He is, after all, a saint. But Jimmy the Saint achieves neither earthly no heavenly glory. Instead, he drives his motorcycle into a hurricane where he dies, "and there's nothin' left but some blood where that body fell, that is, nothin' left that you could sell." The language is unforgiving. Bound for an inglorious death, Jimmy's remains are immediately assessed for their monetary value, which is negligible.

Like the Gunner's, Jimmy the Saint's death involves a misidentification that the singer tries to correct. When a boy approaches the wreckage, the singer says, "Hey kid, you think that's oil? That ain't oil that's blood." The parallel between Jimmy and the Gunner is reinforced in so far as it is not clear what motivates their (ultimately fatal) actions. The singer wonders whether the Gunner has "thrown [his] senses to the war, or [did he] lose them in the flood?" while of Jimmy he asks, "I wonder what he was thinking when he hit that storm, or was he just lost in the flood?" In both scenes, the singer's voice offers a modicum of sanity. At least he can tell the difference between quicksand and mud, between oil and blood; he possesses the wherewithal to question Gunner and Jimmy as they advance toward their respective deaths.

The third scene is a firefight between a Bronx gang and the New York Police. It opens calmly, the singer strolling along Eighth Avenue where he encounters "some storefront incarnation of Maria, she's putting on me

---

[13] "This Train" is discussed in "Riders on the Train," the note following chapter five.

the stare." Now, *incarnation* commonly refers to the Christian doctrine that God was incarnated, made flesh, in the form of Jesus Christ. It is, however, not God incarnate that the singer encounters, but Mary ("Maria" in that predominantly Spanish-speaking part of the Bronx), standing in a storefront and suggestively gazing at him. The Virgin Mary is incarnated in a Bronx prostitute, or, at the very least, a frankly sexual woman.[14]And if this is Mary, it is no surprise that the "Bronx's best apostle" is not a disciple of Christ who goes forth to proclaim the Good News, but rather a gang leader standing "with his hand on his own hardware." A firefight with the police ensues and, like his predecessors in the song, the Bronx's best apostle suffers a meaningless death. A second burst of violence follows as a young man rushes the police but is shot in the leg and falls to the ground. In response, an unnamed bystander notes that "his body hit the street with such a beautiful thud," reducing the horror of the young man's shooting to a moment of aesthetic pleasure, a comment analogous to the earlier statement that Jimmy the Saint's death produced "nothing left that you could sell." Jimmy's death is framed in commercial terms, the Bronx man's shooting in aesthetic terms; both statements deny the basic humanity of the dead and the wounded.

This second shooting effects a subtle but significant shift. In the two previous scenes, the singer tried to confront the violence, warning the Gunner against entering the quicksand and telling the confused young man that the liquid on the highway is not oil but blood. Both are tentative (and, in the Gunner's case, ineffective) gestures that, in a morally grounded world, would not count for much. But against the backdrop of defiled nuns and suicidal saints, the singer's modest attempts at correcting the errors of his fellow men stand out. It is, then, a sign of despair that the singer describes the man just shot by the police as lying in the street, clutching his leg and screaming in Spanish, "still breathing when I walked away." The horror of this statement is concentrated in the word *still*. "Still breathing" implies the man may not be breathing in the

---

[14] It is possible that the Mary in question is Mary Magdalene, who has traditionally been represented (through conflation with the sinful woman of Luke 7:36-50) as a repentant prostitute. However, the song's consistent portrait of the world as a perversion of biblical ideals suggests that it is the Virgin Mary who becomes the prostitute.

very near future: he lies on the ground screaming in pain, bleeding out and perhaps near death. Yet the singer nonchalantly walks away, and the song ends forebodingly—the singer too is now lost in the flood.

There remains a final biblical element to examine, namely, the allusion to the flood narrative in the song's title. Given the grim tone of the song, it is apt that it invokes the biblical story that represents the nadir of God's relationship with humanity, and a steep descent from the positive depiction of the world at creation. As God transforms the dark void into an ordered cosmos, God repeatedly takes stock of the situation and finds it to be good: "And God saw that the light was good" (Genesis 1:4); "God called the dry land Earth, and the waters that were gathered together he called seas. And God saw that it was good" (Genesis 1:10); and similarly with the vegetation, the heavenly bodies, the fish, the birds, and the land creatures—all are judged to be good. Finally, gazing upon creation in its totality, "God saw everything that he had made, and indeed, it was *very* good" (Genesis 1:31). Despite this initial burst of optimism, things unravel quickly: Adam and Eve eat the forbidden fruit, Cain murders his brother, Abel, and God realizes "that the wickedness of humankind was great in the earth, and that every inclination of the thoughts of their hearts was only evil continually. And the Lord was sorry that he had made humankind on the earth, and it grieved him to his heart" (Genesis 6:5-6). In the course of ten generations, the glory of a creation that God deemed "very good" has become a source of divine grief and, shockingly, regret. When God brings a flood upon the world, destroying all the human race with the exception of one family, it is an expression of the world's depravity, and near irredeemability, and in this regard a fitting analogue to the world Springsteen portrays in "Lost in the Flood."

But there is a key difference between the biblical account and Springsteen's song. In Genesis, the flood is a harsh punitive act, but it is also a corrective, wiping the slate clean and allowing for a new beginning. Despite its terrible violence and destruction, the story of Noah ends hopefully, with a covenant "that never again shall all flesh be cut off by the waters of a flood" (Genesis 9:11), and a new beginning in God's instructions to Noah and his sons to "be fruitful and multiply, and fill the earth" (Genesis 9:1). These words hark back to the creation of Adam and Eve, demonstrating that despite its unspeakable horror, the Noah narrative represents a new creation.[15] "Lost in the Flood," in contrast, ends in despair, as the singer capitulates to the unrelenting inhumanity engulfing him.

"Mary Queen of Arkansas" *(Greetings from Asbury Park, N.J.)*

"Mary Queen of Arkansas" is shot through with a tension between the heavenly and earthly realms. This tension first appears in the song's title, that, as Spencer Allen has noted, plays on one of the most common Catholic epithets for the Virgin Mother, "Mary Queen of Heaven."[16] The first three words of the title lead the hearer to expect an ascent toward the heavenly, but these expectations are confounded once Mary's queendom is revealed: Mary Queen of … Arkansas. This frustrated ascent highlights how intractably distant the earthly realm is from the divine, a motif that recurs in the opening stanza:

> Mary queen of Arkansas, it's not too early for dreamin'
> The sky is grown with cloud seed sown and a bastard's love
> can be redeeming
> Mary, my queen, your soft hulk is reviving
> No, you're not too late to desecrate, the servants are just rising

A relatively straightforward reading of the enigmatic second line might identify "cloud seed" either as the process of cloud seeding or

---

[15] See Michael Fishbane, *Biblical Text and Texture: A Literary Reading of Selected Texts* (New York: Schocken, 1979), 33. I thank Ben Sommer for referring me to this source.

[16] Spencer L. Allen, "Mary Queen of Arkansas; Mary Queen of Heaven." Allen's discussion of "Mary Queen of Arkansas" is brief, but I found one comment dismaying: "Though both are defined in primarily sexual terms, Mary, the perpetual virgin and yet mother of Jesus, and Mary Magdalene, the penitent whore, provide the church with a full range of perceptions toward women" (page 6 of printout). This statement suggests that perceptions of women are defined exclusively in sexual terms, such that a virgin, on one end of the spectrum, and a whore, on the other, constitute the "full range." If this is the force of Allen's statement, it is offensive both to characterize women in this manner, and to suggest that the Church does so.

perhaps a poetic characterization of the clouds as seeds that bring rain; and the apparently unrelated reference to a "bastard's love" as a self-deprecating attempt at wooing Mary—the singer knows he is a bastard, but perhaps his love is redeeming all the same. But the line is open to a theological interpretation as well. The sky-seed evokes the Virgin Mary's non-carnal, heavenly insemination that resulted in the redemptive love of a bastard, Jesus, who was conceived before Mary and Joseph were married and is in any case not Joseph's biological son. The two interpretations hang in the balance, until the subsequent line tilts the scales decisively toward the earthly. "Mary, my queen, your soft hulk is reviving" underscores her carnality, and though "revive" means "return to life," the song has no truck with sacred resurrection. Whatever sanctity might have been implied is quickly effaced by the claim that she is "not too late to desecrate."

The subsequent stanzas reinforce the fallen state of the singer and Mary. The singer asserts that he "was not born to live to die," that is, not born to a life of martyrdom, and that Mary's "white skin is deceiving," because "you wake and wait to lie in bait and you almost got me believin'. But on your bed, Mary, I can see the shadow of a noose." These are difficult lines, but a few elements are relatively clear and may provide a vista to the passage as a whole. Mary's white skin is deceiving and the singer is almost convinced by it, but he recoils after seeing a shadow of a noose over her bed. Piecing these elements together, it appears that the singer was tempted to see his lover's body (her white skin) as a way of overcoming the noose, of overcoming death, but the sight of the noose disabuses him of this illusion. If this is correct, the singer's vision of his lover is a further iteration of the song's frustrated-ascent dynamic. He was tempted to believe the love of a woman might offer him a path toward some form of salvation, but finds that no such path exists—the noose over his lover's bed is a reminder of the couple's mortality.

The final stanza presents the singer fully resigned to his this-worldly fate, telling Mary that he has contacts in Mexico and urging her to follow him there, where he will (of course) begin a new life. The song offers no theological redemption, and, ultimately, even the redemptive power of an honest day's work eludes the singer's grasp.[17]

"If I Was the Priest" (not the real title)

There is no proper way to refer to this song, an unreleased track that Bruce Springsteen played for Columbia Records executive John Hammond in 1972 before he was signed to the label.[18] It is clear that "If I Was the Priest" is not correct. In a 1973 interview, Ed Sciaky, a DJ at WMMR in Philadelphia and an early Springsteen booster, referred to the song as "If I Was the Priest." Springsteen rejected that title, and Sciaky asked what it is called. Springsteen replied: "It has no name."[19] In light of this assertion, I will refer to the song as "If I Was the Priest" as shorthand for "the song that has come to be known as 'If I Was the Priest' though Springsteen disavowed that title."

The song opens with an image of otherworldly beckoning: "There's a light on yonder mountain and it's calling me to shine," a phrase that draws on two well-known motifs of light. One, from Jesus' Sermon on the Mount, "you are the light of the world … No one, after lighting a lamp, puts it under the bushel basket ... let your light shine before others" (Matthew 5:14-16). The other, ultimately rooted in the Sermon on the Mount as well, is the 1920's gospel song "This Little Light of Mine," that became a gospel and folk classic, and was later an important song in the Civil Rights movement.[20] But the spiritual tone of the opening line

---

[17] A number of readers have suggested that Mary is a drag queen, largely on the basis of the concluding line of the second stanza: "You're not man enough for me to hate, or woman enough for kissing" (see Kirkpatrick, *Magic in the Night*, 20). The deceptiveness of Mary's white skin might, on this reading, be related to gender ambiguity. I am not convinced by this reading— why would a noose dissuade the singer from believing Mary is biologically female? — but in any case it does not preclude the theological interpretation I have offered.

[18] See the discussion in Kirkpatrick, *Magic in the Night*, 17.

[19] Ed Sciaky, WMMR interview, November 3, 1973; reprinted in Phillips and Masur, *Talk About a Dream*, 27. Allan Clarke, lead singer of The Hollies, recorded the song as "If I Were the Priest" on his 1974 album *Allan Clarke*, but the American version appears to have been *was*. Clarke also released covers of "Born to Run" and "Blinded By the Light" as singles. (Jonathan Cohen, personal communication, informs me that Allan Clarke's version of "If I Was the Priest" also appeared on the collection *One Step Up/Two Steps Back: The Songs of Bruce Springsteen* [Capitol, 1997]).

[20] Springsteen released a version of the song on *Live in Dublin* (Columbia, 2007).

is immediately disrupted by the more earthly attraction of "a girl by the water fountain, and she's asking to be mine." The contrast between the two forces vying for the speaker's attention is stark. The singer does not specify the precise nature of the light, but it calls out to him, inviting him to release the light within himself; the mountain is both a traditional site of divine revelation (Moses on Sinai, Jesus on the mount) and an inspiring vision of nature's glory. The girl, in contrast, is standing by a drinking fountain, a mechanical substitute for natural sources of water and the site of relatively few divine revelations. She is likely in a park, a playground, or a school yard. The shift from the mountain to the fountain is a move from revelation and nature—from the possibility of transcendent experience—to the mechanical and the mundane. Note, finally, the register of the different prepositions: the singer sees the light "on yonder mountain," an archaic, biblically evocative phrase, while the girl is located, quite colloquially, "over by" the water fountain.

Having thematized the disparity between the transcendent and the quotidian, "If I Was the Priest" introduces Jesus and locates him in the latter: "And ain't that Jesus, he's standing in the doorway." The language is informal, the setting manmade, and the tone nonchalant, more off-hand comment than religious revelation. Jesus, as it happens, is a Wild West character, dressed in a buckskin jacket and spurred boots, a style that evidently suits him as the singer finds him to be "so really fine." At this point the song becomes a surreal description of the Holy Family transplanted into a Wild West setting: Jesus is a lawman; the Virgin Mary runs the Holy Grail saloon; and the Holy Ghost is the proprietor of the local burlesque show. Outrageous parody, to be sure, but sophisticated parody that plays on established religious language and motifs. When Jesus tells the singer he is needed "up in Dodge City, son," his language is at once pastoral ("Yes, my son…") and a standard Wild Westernism ("Now, look here, son …"). Which sense of "son" is sheriff-Jesus using when he speaks to the singer? A similar ambiguity attends the characterization of Jesus as a lawman ("we need you up in Dodge City, son, 'cause there's just too many outlaws"). The struggle to bring the American West under the rule of law is a literary and cinematic cliché. But when sheriff-Jesus defends the law, we cannot but think of New Testament passages that cast him as the champion of the law (or: the Law, that is, the Torah). "Do not think I have come to abolish the law or the prophets; I have come not to abolish but to fulfill. For truly I tell you, until heaven and earth pass away, not one letter, not one stroke of a letter, will pass from the law until all is accomplished" (Matthew 5:17-18). Like the address "son," the song parodies the Holy Family by means of Wild West motifs that resonate uncannily with the language of the New Testament.

The reinterpretation of Mary is more brutal. As noted above, she runs "the Holy Grail saloon," and is the embodiment of the Madonna-Whore complex: on Sundays she serves mass, but the next day she sells her body. Springsteen does not pull punches. Mary is a junkie and a boozer, and a terrible prostitute to boot since "she's only been made once or twice, by some kind of magic." In all this, Springsteen continues reworking established religious motifs, sometimes with real subtlety. The Holy Grail is, after all, the chalice Jesus used during the Last Supper, so the eponymous saloon represents a radical secularization of Gospel alcohol. And as I noted in the discussion of "Lost in the Flood," the description of Mary represents an old anti-Christian polemic that Mary's claims of divine conception were intended to obscure her promiscuity.[21] The Holy Ghost (Springsteen calls it "the host with the most," punning on its role as proprietor of an establishment and sacramental host) runs a burlesque show "where they let you in for free, but boy do they hit you when you go"—likely an allusion to the church's riches and the collection plate circulated during Mass; and "big bad Bobby" has been "known to down eleven and then ask for another," the sum equaling the traditional number of Jesus' apostles. As for the singer himself, he complains of having scabs on his knees "from kneeling way too long," a stance he must now renounce in order to rise up and become a man.[22]

---

[21] The claim that Mary's sexual experience was by "some kind of magic" clearly indicates the reference is to Mary the mother of Christ, who was impregnated by the Holy Spirit, and not to Mary Magdalene.

[22] Note the evolution of the motif of callused or scabbed knees from the 1968 fragment discussed in the opening of this chapter ("Jesus, Joseph, and Mary ...").

Though extreme in its formulations, "If I Was the Priest" is typical of the openly critical stand a number of Springsteen's earlier songs take toward traditional Christian institutions and beliefs. Typical in that the critique comes from "within," playing on Christian and especially Catholic images, and typical too in its thorough debasement of these images. Saints are shown to be sinners, sinners to be saints, traditional paths to salvation lead to perdition, and venerated figures are recast as shady characters. But to what end? One obvious answer is that these early songs are a form of rebellion—Springsteen is breaking away from his Catholic upbringing and expressing his anger through these harsh works. I have no doubt that this explanation is true, so far as it goes, but the religious critique of the songs discussed here serves a constructive role as well: it clears the way for a non-traditional, immanent path to redemption.

CHAPTER TWO

The Profane Sanctified

Born to Run … to me is like religiously based … Not like orthodox religion, but it's about basic things, you know? That searchin', and faith, and the idea of hope.[1]

Springsteen's early critique of traditional religion is fierce and bitter, but it does not entail an unqualified rejection of traditional religious ideals. Much as Grace Paley refashioned the Psalm tradition into a vehicle for the glorification of the two young butchers, and Czeslaw Milosz created an intermediate space that allows the transcendent to be manifested within the immanent world, significant parts of Springsteen's early works seek to transcribe religious categories into this-worldly reality. A song like "Sister Theresa," discussed in the previous chapter, hints at such a possibility when it suggests the titular nun would be better off ending her

[1] Kurt Loder, "The *Rolling Stone* Interview: Bruce Springsteen," *Rolling Stone*, December 6, 1984; reprinted in *Bruce Springsteen: The* Rolling Stone *Files* (New York: Hyperion, 1996), 155.

spiritual commitment to Christ and opting instead for a carnal relationship with the singer. Redemption is not found in Church doctrine, but rather in physical intimacy. "Sister Theresa" does not make this claim, but it does suggest how a critique of traditional religion might be a constitutive element of an alternate, immanent, understanding of redemption.

"Does this Bus Stop at 82nd Street?" *(Greetings from Asbury Park, NJ)*

Springsteen peppers his early songs with references to a grace that resides in the world. "Does This Bus Stop at 82nd Street?" is a joyful song about a New York bus ride that opens with the singer telling the driver to "bless your children, give them names," and then offering "drink this and you'll grow wings on your feet." The drink itself is never identified, but it portrays the world as a place populated by bus drivers, among others, who can fly. The song revisits the flight motif with a scene of heavenly ascent in the third stanza:

> Mary Lou she found out how to cope
> She rides to the heavens on a gyroscope
> The *Daily News* asked her for the dope
> She said, "Man, the dope's that there's still hope"

Like the wing-producing elixir, Mary Lou's gyroscope may well be a drug, but the playful lines that follow indicate that, even if it is, she aims higher. The *Daily News*' request "for the dope" is ambiguous: the journalistic context suggests *dope* is information, while Mary Lou's ecstatic experience suggests *dope* is her drug of choice. Mary Lou's answer—"the dope is that there's still hope"—maintains this ambiguity, for she could be referring to the information, or characterizing a mood-altering substance as hope. In either case, it is an uplifting response. Hope fuels her ascent to the heavens. So while neither Mary Lou nor the bus driver actually enters the divine realm, they inhabit a world that allows them to take flight and even reach heavenly heights.

"Spirit in the Night" *(Greetings from Asbury Park, NJ)*

"Spirit in the Night" describes a romantic Saturday night trip in divine (but still this-worldly) terms. Billy, one of the singer's friends, describes Greasy Lake, the destination, as a gathering place for angels: "I'll take you all out to where the gypsy angels go, they're built like light and they dance like spirits in the night." When the group reaches Greasy Lake, the singer and Janey dance all night, and the song again employs angel imagery, when she kisses him "like only a lonely angel can." Transformation into an angelic figure, a spirit, could draw on the New Testament distinction between the material and the spiritual—a rejection of earthly garb due to the desire to be, in Paul's words, "clothed with our heavenly dwelling" (2 Corinthians 5:2).[2] But Janey remains a physical spirit, a carnal angel, finding companionship in a kiss and holding the hands of the man who will soon become her lover. The traditional opposition of the spiritual and the carnal is rejected, for it is precisely because Janey and the singer are open to physical joy that is innocent and spontaneous that they achieve true spirituality, fully expressed in the couple's lovemaking: "Me and Crazy Janey was makin' love in the dirt, singin' our birthday song." Locating the lovers in the dirt does not mean that their love is dirty, because, crucially, they are singing their *birthday song*, the "song" each sang at birth. Their nakedness has been transformed into a redemptive force; they are naked and crying out like newborns, having recovered the innocence of Eden on the shores of Greasy Lake.[3]

---

[2] The relevance of 2 Corinthians to this discussion was suggested to me by Ben Sommer.

[3] The permeability of the heavenly and earthly realms is also evidenced by the regular presence of fallen angels in songs such as "Drive All Night," "Racing in the Street," and more. "So Young and In Love," a *Born to Run* outtake released on *Tracks*, opens with the lines: "There's flying angels on your fire escape; They lie to your mama for you, try to keep you safe." The angels—*flying* angels, no less—are hanging out on the fire escape, helping the young man sneak out to see his love. Early versions of "4th of July, Asbury Park (Sandy)" include the line "Well, now, Sandy, them north side angels, they lost their desire for us; I spoke with 'em last night, they said they won't set themselves on fire for us anymore" (versus the studio version: "Well, Sandy, the waitress I was seeing lost her desire for me; I spoke with her last night she said she won't set herself on fire for me anymore"). I thank Lou Masur for this reference.

"Resurrection"

While "Does This Bus Stop at 82nd Street?" and "Spirit in the Night" refer to moments of grace within the world, neither song foregrounds its theological concerns. More theologically explicit is "Resurrection," a song that dates back to the time when Springsteen performed with the band Steel Mill.[4] The song portrays the religious conflict of a young man who admits to knowing "the devil too well," and while he has not broken with his faith altogether ("Well, I can't say I'm a believer, I can't say that I ain't"), his attitude toward the church is unquestionably critical. His mother is convinced he is going to burn in hell and drags him to church every Sunday, but the rituals and teachings strike him as empty, more commercial transaction than spiritual experience: "And we confess our sins, special old price of three Hail Marys and your soul is clean again." The sisters' instruction is, moreover, frankly dogmatic: "You must believe what we are saying to believe for without belief you are dying." Here the narrative shifts and the singer launches into a chorus, "hail, hail, resurrection, you're all invited to come and dance on my grave," followed by four repetitions of the phrase "I'll say my prayers to the earth and the sun,"[5] then seven repetitions of "hail, hail resurrection." Clearly, the singer is no longer criticizing church practices, and has turned to embrace some form of worship of the natural world.

The word *resurrection* is key. The chorus "hail, hail, resurrection" and the line "you're all invited to dance on my grave" appear to invoke the Christian doctrine of Christ's physical return from the dead. But while the singer employs language drawn from church theology, a number of considerations militate against a Christological reading. The lines preceding the chorus are all in the first person, as is the subsequent phrase "I'll say my prayers to the earth and sun," so "my grave" is spoken by the singer, not Jesus. Also, the first part of the song criticizes church

[4] According to http://www.brucespringsteen.it/DB/sd3.aspx?sid=463, Steel Mill recorded "Resurrection" in early 1970. That track was lost, but a bootleg recording from a live performance exists.

[5] The line "Oh, I'm gonna have a lot of money" appears between the opening of the stanza and the fourfold repetition.

teachings, so a celebration of Christ's resurrection would represent a return to the ecclesiastical fold, contrary to the song's broader message. To the contrary, the chorus is part of a shift toward a different, nature-oriented religiosity. However, if we take the first person voice seriously, we must conclude that it is that of the singer throughout, and that he is inviting people to dance on his grave and witness his resurrection—an implausible interpretation, at least at first blush. But the singer *has* died from the perspective of the nuns' statement that without belief in their doctrines "you are dying." In that case, says the singer, I invite you to come dance on my grave—for I will not accept the doctrines you claim give life, and so the singer "dies" in refusing the church's doctrines, but is resurrected when he offers prayers to the earth and the sun. If so, "Resurrection" makes a robust theological claim: it uproots the cycle of death-and-resurrection from its traditional, Christological context, and recasts the singer's own death (in the eyes of the nuns) and resurrection into a form of nature-worship—his prayers to the earth and the sun with their strong pagan resonance.[6] "Resurrection" reframes the core church doctrine as the singer's own rebirth achieved, ironically, through the rejection of the church.

"Thunder Road" *(Born to Run)*

To this point, I have identified two related strands in Springsteen's early work: a critique of traditional religious concepts, and an attempt to reinterpret these concepts in immanent, this-worldly terms. "Thunder Road" manifests the two positions in the dialogue of its protagonists, identifying Mary, the song's female character, with traditional religious salvation, the male singer with its immanent substitute.7 The song

[6] One could argue that the song reintroduces the pagan views of resurrection that informed the early Christian doctrine. For an accessible survey of pagan teachings on the subject see Christopher Bryan, *The Resurrection of the Messiah* (New York and Oxford: Oxford University Press, 2011), 19-34.

[7] Kate McCarthy anticipates parts of my argument in "Deliver Me from Nowhere: Bruce Springsteen and the Myth of the American Promised Land," in Eric Michael Mazur and Kate McCarthy, editors, *God in the Details: American Religion in Popular Culture* (New York and London: Routledge, 2000), 23-45.

is a sustained attempt to woo Mary, an ethereal figure whom we first encounter as she dances across the porch "like a vision."[8] As the song unfolds, it becomes apparent that Mary stands for religious practices and beliefs that the singer opposes, and he understands his task as redirecting her from her current spiritual trajectory:

> You can hide 'neath your covers
> And study your pain
> Make crosses from your lovers
> Throw roses in the rain
> Waste your summers praying in vain
> For a savior to rise from these streets

Making crosses from her lovers, Mary arguably casts them in the role of Christ-like martyrs and metaphorically crucifies them, or perhaps she uses them as penance for her transgressions. In either case, she links her lovers with the image of Christ on the cross, and the singer is critical of this juxtaposition. The roses are a traditional symbol for the Virgin Mary, already attested in early Christian sources.[9] In the Song of Songs, the man praises his lover as "a lily among the thorns" (Song of Songs 2:2) and as "a garden locked is my sister, my bride, a garden locked, a fountain sealed" (4:12). In later interpretive traditions, the biblical lily was identified with the rose, and the image of the sealed garden understood as a reference to Mary's virginity.[10] Thus, the fourth-century bishop Saint Ambrose speaks of Mary as the "rose of modesty," and many medieval hymns refer to the Virgin Mary as the "rose of heaven," "the eternal rose," and the like.[11] As a result, Mary's apparitions came to be identified with roses, as

[8] Though much has been made of the name Mary, I am unsure how much symbolic weight it can bear on its own. In earlier versions of "Thunder Road," the woman is named either Christie or Angelina, and there may be prosodic or compositional reasons for preferring Mary. Far more significant, is the character's link with Marian imagery (see below).

[9] See Anne Winston-Allen, *Stories of the Rose: The Making of the Rosary in the Middle Ages* (University Park, PA: Pennsylvania State University Press, 1997).

[10] This shift, attested as early as the 5th century Christian poet Sedulius, may be due to the prominence of the rose in Greek and Roman symbolism, as well as the fact that the rose has thorns and so accords with the Song of Song's flower "among the thorns."

[11] On St. Ambrose see Winston-Allen, *Stories of the Rose*, 88. For an overview of the incorporation

when the thirteenth century St. Elizabeth of Hungary distributed food to the poor against her father's instructions, but when she was caught, the prohibited bread miraculously disappeared and her basket was filled with roses. A similar miracle occurred to her grand-niece, St. Elizabeth of Portugal.[12] Over a century later, the 1531 apparition of the Virgin Mary to a peasant in the Mexican town of Guadalupe was marked by the spontaneous growth of Castilian roses, a plant not native to the New World. The association of Mary with the rose also underpins the claim that the Peruvian Isabel Flores y de Oliva (1586-1617) was transfigured into the image of a rose in infancy, as well as her decision to take the name Rose at the time of her confirmation. A lay member of the Dominican order, she would eventually become known as St. Rose of Lima, the first Catholic saint born in the New World. Perhaps not coincidentally, St. Rose of Lima was also the namesake of the Catholic school Springsteen attended through eighth grade, where he was surrounded by images of the Virgin Mary, St. Rose of Lima, and roses. When Mary (the song's character) tosses roses in the rain, she is symbolically expressing her hope for a divine apparition.

Mary's desire to hide beneath her covers and study her pain suggests that her choices are driven by childlike fear and a cultivated sense of victimhood. Mary retreats from the physical world and the risks it entails, and has in the past chosen men who mirror this attitude, as we see in the description of her former lovers:

> There were ghosts in the eyes of all the boys you sent away
> They haunt this dusty beach road
> In the skeleton frames of burned out Chevrolets
> They scream your name at night in the street
> [...]
> But when you get to the porch they're gone on the wind

---

of Pagan rose imagery into Christian sources see Lisa Cucciniello, "Rose to Rosary: The Flower of Venus in Catholicism" in Frankie Hutton, editor, *Rose Lore: Essays in Cultural History and Semiotics* (Lanham, MD: Rowan and Littlefield, 2008), 63-91.

[12] On St. Elizabeth of Hungary and St. Elizabeth of Portugal, see Edward and Laura Mornin, *Saints: A Visual Guide* (Grand Rapids, MI: Eerdmans, 2006), 222 and 234, respectively.

The scene is one of disembodied existence. The rejected boys have ghosts in their eyes—perhaps the reflection of vision-like Mary, perhaps other ghosts—and they too become ghosts, haunting the road outside her house. Their cries bespeak a desire for Mary, but when she steps out to the porch, "they're gone on the wind." These yearning specters, fleeing as the object of their desire draws near, mirror Mary herself—her ethereal presence, her desire for a saintly savior, and her hesitation in the face of the flesh-and-blood singer, who stands as the polar opposite of her former suitors. He is explicit about his emotional needs. Roy Orbison's "For the Lonely" elicits a confession of his own loneliness, and he implores Mary "don't turn me home again I just can't face myself alone again." He is also explicit about his desire for her—"darlin' you know just what I'm here for." He is a man and there is no need to spell out the sexual aspect of his wooing.

At this point we might be tempted to frame the division between Mary and the singer in terms of spirit versus body, the religious versus the earthly; to describe "Thunder Road" as a later iteration of "Sister Theresa," where the singer tries to draw a pious woman into the pleasures of the flesh. But "Thunder Road" resists such an interpretation, as we first see in the singer's request that Mary "show a little faith ... there's magic in the night." At first glance, the request appears paradoxical, since faith is precisely what Mary is showing, with her roses, and her crosses, and her summer spent in prayer. But as the song progresses it becomes evident that the singer does not wish to eliminate Mary's faith, but rather to redirect it from the transcendent realm of traditional religion to the more modest redemptive promise of the immanent world.

While the singer takes Mary to task for praying for a savior to rise from the streets, he does not deny salvation altogether: "All the redemption I can offer girl is beneath this dirty hood." The dirty hood of a car may appear an odd place to encounter redemption, yet that is where the singer stakes his claim—in the mundane world, with all its gritty imperfection. To be clear, he is not trying to compete with the savior for whom Mary pines, noting "now I'm no hero, that's understood." But while Mary considers imperfection a sign of weakness, for the singer it signifies freedom from unrealistic expectations, freedom to accept the diminished salvation that is available to them. This is why he calls attention to her imperfection, and immediately proclaims his acceptance of it: "you ain't a beauty, but, hey, you're all right, and that's all right with me." Proclaiming that a woman "ain't a beauty" may be a dubious wooing technique, but the singer is not only trying to bed Mary (though he is doing that too); he is also encouraging her to make peace with her imperfection, with her humanity. Mary's fear that "maybe we ain't that young anymore" is followed by the singer's exhortation to show a little faith despite—and without denying—their mortality, their fallenness. For there is yet magic in the night, in the man standing before her, and though the redemption he promises is diminished, it is redemption nonetheless.

The singer makes explicit both the promise and its limits when he tells Mary "we've got one last chance to make it real, to trade in these wings on some wheels."[13] Wings, and the angelic associations they conjure, are certainly a loftier mode of transportation, and understandably exert a powerful draw on Mary. It is a sign of the maturity of "Thunder Road" that the song acknowledges the loss that Mary will incur if she does trade in the wings for wheels. To relinquish the beliefs that have sustained Mary thus far comes with a clear cost, as "the door is open but the ride ain't free." Mary will have to make peace with the fact that her lover is no hero, that he offers her wheels instead of wings. But the singer exhorts her to adopt his vision all the same, because to trade wings for wheels is "to make it real." Better an imperfect real salvation than a perfect, unattainable one.

The next line spells out one aspect of making it real, when the singer asks Mary to "climb in back, heaven's waiting down on the tracks." In his discussion of "Thunder Road," Jeffrey Symynkywicz calls the reader's attention to the phrase "from your front porch to my front seat," stating: "Mary is not being beckoned to the young man's *back seat*, with all the predictable messiness that back seats connote."[14] But Symynkywicz is

---

[13] "At the February 5 show at the Main Point in Bryn Mawr, Springsteen premiered 'Wings for Wheels,' which would evolve into 'Thunder Road'," Lou Masur, *Runaway Dream:* Born to Run *and Bruce Springsteen's American Vision* (New York: Bloomsbury, 2009), 52.

[14] Jeffrey Symynkywicz, *The Gospel According to Bruce Springsteen*, 28; emphasis in the original.

only partially correct. The singer does not beckon her *only* into the back seat, but "climb in back" suggests that the back seat (and its attendant "messiness") has a share of heaven, as well. Of course, the association of sex and heaven is a rock 'n' roll commonplace that typically does not merit theological analysis. In "Thunder Road," however, it is part of a sustained attempt to replace the transcendent promises of religious salvation with immanent counterparts. To liken sex with heaven is not only a way of extolling its pleasures; it is a claim that love—and lust—between a couple is a type of heaven available in the real world.

The song's ambivalence about the scope of its own salvific claims is highlighted in the singer's paradoxical exhortation that Mary take his hand so they can "case the Promised Land." To "case" something is to examine it in preparation for theft: a thief cases the jewels she plans to lift, or the bank she plans to rob. As Ben Sommer insightfully notes, the need to case the Promised Land indicates that it was not promised to that person. That is, the singer identifies himself as a member of the Unchosen People, someone who was never supposed to make it into the Promised Land but rather was destined for "the working life" of *Darkness on the Edge of Town*.[15] At the same time, the idea of casing the Promised Land also reflects the theological tension that runs through "Thunder Road." The singer offers an alternate doctrine of salvation, and toward that end reinterprets key religious terms: faith is no longer placed in the teachings of the Church, but in the magic of the night; redemption is not brought about through the agency of a savior, but through the revving of the engine under the dirty hood of a car; heaven is not a spiritual realm, but carnal pleasures experienced in the back seat; angels' wings give way to wheels.[16] The singer introduces the Promised Land motif because it represents a secular parallel to the biblical destination, but the song's immanent doctrine of salvation does not allow for divine promises, so God cannot be the guarantor of Mary's and the singer's

[15] Ben Sommer, personal communication.

[16] As Springsteen would say three decades later: "[Thunder Road] was my invitation to my audience, to myself ... my invitation to a long and earthly, very earthly journey," *Bruce Springsteen: VH1 Storytellers*, directed by David Diomedi (2005; Rutherford, NJ: Sony Legacy), at the 1:35 mark.

redemption. There may be a Promised Land, but it is not provided by God. The Promised Land of "Thunder Road" is created by our decisions, our actions. We may take possession of it eventually, but only after first casing it.

"Night" and "Born to Run" *(Born to Run)*

It is no coincidence that George Yamin, in the first academic essay to discuss Springsteen's theology, focuses on the street and night as sites of redemption.[17] In "Thunder Road" and "Born to Run" in particular, Yamin argues, we see that "the car (or motorcycle) is for Springsteen a symbol of great religious importance, for it is a literal vehicle of salvation that facilitates one's passage from his original point of departure to his final goal."[18] No song on *Born to Run* is as explicitly theological as "Thunder Road," but both "Night" and the title track celebrate the same salvific trinity of woman, night, and open road, while casting the travails of the day as a backdrop to the freedom that comes at sundown.[19] "Born to Run" merely gestures toward the bleakness of daytime ("In the day we sweat it out on the streets of a runaway American dream") as a foil to the liberating abandon of the night. The contrast between night and day is more emphatic in "Night," with the singer waking up to the sound of the work bell and suffering his boss' wrath, a daily form of oppression that dissipates only once you're out driving at night: "you work nine to five and somehow you survive till the night."

---

[17] Yamin, "The Theology of Bruce Springsteen," especially 4-11.

[18] Yamin, "The Theology of Bruce Springsteen," 10.

[19] Springsteen's writing, in particular his early works, has come under criticism for its portrayal of women as, first and foremost, facilitators of male redemption. For a clear statement of this critique see Pamela Moss, "Still Searching for the Promised Land: Placing Women in Bruce Springsteen's Lyrical Landscapes," *Cultural Geographies* 18 (2011), 343-362; see also the sources Lisa Zitelli cites and to which she responds, in "'Like a Vision She Dances': Re-Visioning the Female Figure in the Songs of Bruce Springsteen," in Harde and Streight, *Reading the Boss: Interdisciplinary Approaches to the Works of Bruce Springsteen*, 151-173. There is no question that Springsteen writes almost exclusively from a male perspective, the handful of exceptions incudes: "A Good Man is Hard to Find (Pittsburgh)," a *Born in the U.S.A.* outtake; "Car Wash," a *Nebraska* outtake; and "My Lover Man," a *Human Touch* outtake—all three released on *Tracks*.

Once the workday is done, both "Born to Run" and "Night" shift their focus to women and the open road. "Born to Run," like "Thunder Road," is addressed to a woman, Wendy, whom the singer hopes will join him, though the destination of their shared drive is unknown. "Someday," he promises her, they will "get to that place where we really want to go." The drive is first and foremost an escape from their present situation, and only much farther down the road a hoped-for arrival at an ultimate destination. In "Night," the woman is herself the destination ("you'll find her somehow, you swear"), but driving is in any case salvific:[20]

> ... with faith in your machine
> Off you scream into the night
> And you're in love with all the wonder it brings
> And every muscle in your body sings
> As the highway ignites

As Lou Masur has noted, "[t]he line evokes Walt Whitman in 'I Sing the Body Electric.' If the daytime work experience is physically exhausting ... the nighttime is physically liberating, allowing you to 'break on through' to a different state of being, if only for a short time."[21]

Taken together, "Thunder Road," "Night," and "Born to Run" stand as the positive complement to the critique in *Greetings from Asbury Park, N.J.* The old doctrines and institutions have lost their vitality; there is no use in waiting for redemption to descend from the heavens. But this new reality is not cause for despair. To the contrary, in recognizing it we pave the way for a new, immanent salvation, animated by "a belief in an ideal world that lies both literally and figuratively at the end of the road on which driver and passenger travel."[22] The road is neither easy nor always joyous, and Lou Masur rightly reminds us that "[s]adness and despair haunt the album, even in its most triumphal moments."[23] Still, many of

---

[20] The singer presumably drives in illegal street races, that he refers to as "the circuits."

[21] Masur, *Runaway Dream*, 77.

[22] Yamin, "The Theology of Bruce Springsteen," 9-10.

[23] Masur, *Runaway* Dream, 77. The ecstatic nighttime drive in "Night" ends in a melancholy vow that "you'll run sad and free," and the singer of "Born to Run" promises that "together, Wendy, we can live with the sadness. "Jungleland" and "Meeting Across the River" are darker still.

Born to Run's tracks explode with a centrifugal energy, with the promise that escape is possible: "we gotta get out while we're young," "these two lanes will take us anywhere," and "you run sad and free until all you can see is the night."[24] The album's mobility, the possibility of escaping the city for the open road, is tantamount to a gospel of this-worldly redemption. And many became believers. *Born to Run* was a turning point in Springsteen's career, transforming him from a respected but not widely known musician, to an artistic and commercial icon, fulfilling in a very short time Jon Landau's famous assertion that he had seen the "rock and roll future and its name is Bruce Springsteen."[25] And yet, after constructing this edifice to such acclaim, Springsteen, remarkably, turned around and tore it down.

---

[24] Quotes are from "Born to Run," "Thunder Road," and "Night," respectively.

[25] Jon Landau, "Growing Young With Rock and Roll," *The Real Paper*, May 22, 1974.

CHAPTER THREE

Toward the Apocalypse

I wanted [*Darkness on the Edge of Town*] to have a sort of apocalyptic grandeur[1]

The theological elements in the albums that precede *Darkness on the Edge of Town* form, I have argued, a coherent structure, one component of which is a critique of traditional religious (especially Catholic) symbols and institutions; the meaning of the symbols is inverted and the institutions shown to be spiritually hollow. A second, corollary, component transposes the promise of traditional religion into the immanent world, maintaining the possibility of redemption through romantic love and open highways. The critical component steers the listener away from the Church, while the constructive component points

[1] In Thom Zimny, director, *The Promise: The Making of* Darkness on the Edge of Town (2011), at the 1 hour 10 minute mark. My thanks to Prof. Kennth Campbell of Monmouth University for bringing this video to my attention.

her in the desired direction. *Darkness on the Edge of Town* methodically dismantles these claims. Much as the preceding albums did for traditional Church teachings, *Darkness on the Edge of Town* both critiques the salvific claims of *Born to Run* and offers an alternate religious paradigm—that of the apocalypse.[2]

The critique of *Born to Run* is evident in the opening lines of *Darkness on the Edge of Town* (from the song "Badlands"), that inform us nothing remains as it was:

> Lights out tonight
> Trouble in the heartland
> Got a head-on collision
> Smashin' in my guts, man

Any listener who believed that *Darkness on the Edge of Town* would continue the trajectory established in *Born to Run* is immediately disabused of that notion. In the earlier album, *lights out* would mark a moment of liberation when the singers steps out into the night either with or in search of a woman; here, *lights out* indicates "trouble in the heartland," and in lieu of a redemptive drive, a "head-on collision," as liberating mobility cedes to a violent crash. In four short lines, the album announces: the old order is gone.

Of course, a number of constants remain.[3] The men that populate *Darkness on the Edge of Town* are as fallen as their predecessors, as haunted by the realization that their lives are inadequate to their aspirations. They are painfully aware that "there's so much that you want, you deserve

---

[2] Many writers have linked the darker tone of this album to the legal dispute between Springsteen and his then-manager, Mike Appel. Whatever its merits, this biographical claim does not have any bearing on the specifically theological transformation that I survey here. Note that discussion of "Adam Raised a Cain" is deferred to chapter seven ("Springsteen's Midrash").

[3] The break between *Darkness on the Edge of Town* and *Born to Run* is not absolute. "Prove It All Night," a guardedly optimistic song on *Darkness on the Edge of Town*, is of a piece with *Born to Run*. The pessimism of the later album is, moreover, continuous with the darker songs on *Born to Run*, such as "Meeting Across the River" and "Jungleland." The key difference remains that *Born to Run* asserts the *possibility* of redemption, even though it recognizes that no everyone will attain it.

much more than this," and want desperately to "find one place" that will treat them with dignity and respect.[4] Another constant is the futility of work. One singer's "Daddy worked his whole life for nothing but the pain," and another laments the despair of "the working life."[5] But if the albums agree that their characters stand in need of redemption, they differ on what avenues, if any, are open to them. In "The Promise," a song recorded for *Darkness on the Edge of Town* but not released until years later,[6] Springsteen revisits the man driving off into the night and finds him headed toward "dead ends" and "bad scenes," to the point that the singer confesses that he "cashed in a few of my own dreams." The song's revisionist agenda finds explicit expression when the singer invokes "Thunder Road" (the song or the location—it is not clear) as a site of death: "Thunder Road, oh baby you were so right, Thunder Road, there's somethin' dyin' down on the highway tonight." This statement illustrates the shift between the two albums. It is not that *Darkness on the Edge of Town* is about losers and *Born to Run* about winners, it is that *Darkness on the Edge of Town* turns the winners of *Born to Run* into losers.

"Something in the Night" *(Darkness on the Edge of Town)*

A notable example of this transformation: the aspirational dream of "Night" becomes a nightmare in its antithesis, "Something in the Night."[7] The song opens with the singer driving toward a local bar and turning up the volume on the radio "so I don't have to think." The drive is agitating

[4] Quotes are from "Prove It All Night" and "Badlands," respectively.

[5] Quotes are from "Adam Raised a Cain" and "Factory," respectively. The latter is a particularly damning portrait of daily labor. It is true that the factory "gives … life" to its workers, but it is a life of spirit-crushing monotony: "End of the day, factory whistle cries, men walk through these gates with death in their eyes." Symynkywicz's suggestion that the song "praises the unromanticized heroism" of the workers (*The Gospel According to Bruce Springsteen*, 47) is itself unduly romantic.

[6] "The Promise" was released on *The Promise* (Columbia, 2010), a CD of *Darkness on the Edge of Town* outtakes.

[7] In Brent Bellamy's words, "'Something in the Night' subverts everything that *Born to Run* fights for on the level of content and form," "Tear into the Guts: Whitman, Steinbeck, and the Durability of Lost Souls on the Road," *Canadian Review of American Studies/Revue canadienne d'études américaines* 41 (2011), 235-236.

and the singer seeks distraction. Pushing the gas pedal to the floor, he looks "for a moment when the world seems right," that is to say, he is aware of the promise the drive might—and in earlier works would—hold for him. But he never reaches this destination. Instead, he hits a barrier, "[tearing] into the guts of something in the night." The remainder of the song contains grim meditations on the human condition—man comes into the world with nothing and anything gained will be stripped away—and describes a drive that devolves into terror. It begins in loneliness, as the singer rides through the night without seeing another person, "just kids wasted on something in the night." The singer and unnamed companions do, ultimately, find the things they love, but the objects are "crushed and dying." The group (couple?) try to escape but are caught "at the state line" by unidentified assailants who burn their cars and leave them "running burned and blind, chasing something in the night." The song's atmosphere is nightmarish: its characters are nameless, their goals obscure, their enemies faceless. What does emerge clearly is that the car has been stripped of its redemptive power. A drive may proceed aimlessly, never reaching a destination, or it may be brought to a violent stop by an external force, but it cannot lead to the Promised Land.

"Candy's Room" *(Darkness on the Edge of Town)*

"Something in the Night" does not address the salvific power of the woman, and romantic relationships do not feature prominently in *Darkness on the Edge of Town* as a whole,[8] though "Candy's Room" suggests women too have lost their status as a possible path to redemption. In Candy's room "there are pictures of her heroes on the wall," or, according to "Candy's Boy," an earlier version of the song, "a picture of her savior on the wall." In both versions, Candy wants to be saved, be it romantically or religiously, and her statement "baby if you wanna be wild" echoes the desire of the singer in "Born to Run" to "know if love is wild." Candy and the singer appear to experience redemptive love, as he sings of driving deep into the light in her

[8] The lone exception is "Prove It All Night," a sober but optimistic song about the love and struggles of a couple.

eyes and describes the transformative power of their physical love: "When I hold Candy close she makes the hidden worlds mine." But as the song unfolds, we learn that "strangers from the city call my baby's number and they bring her toys," and she knows many men who give her anything she wants. While it is not clear if Candy is, strictly speaking, a prostitute, she clearly maintains a series of materially beneficial relationships with various lovers. And the song is ambiguous throughout as to whether Candy cares about the singer, since when he comes by her house "she smiles pretty, she knows I wanna be Candy's boy," a gesture that has less to do with love than with the image she projects to the men who desire her. It is altogether possible, then, that the singer loves Candy, but that she merely enjoys the company of a man willing to give "all that I got to give" to be with her. Ultimately, "Candy's Room" affirms the singer's belief in redemptive love, but casts doubt on its reality.

"The Iceman" *(Tracks)*

A theologically oriented outtake that deserves mention, "The Iceman" contains many of the elements familiar from *Born to Run*: a young man frustrated in a sleepy town that "ain't got the guts to budge," a young woman to whom the song is addressed, and the promise of a midnight drive. However, the couple is not headed out to the Promised Land; the midnight road leads "right to the devil's door, and even the white angels of Eden with their flamin' swords won't be able to stop us from hittin' town in this dirty old Ford." At first glance, the biblical imagery is confusing. The devil's door suggests they are headed toward hell, but the angels of Eden and their flaming swords are a clear allusion to the celestial guardians of the Garden of Eden:

> Therefore the Lord God sent him forth from the garden of Eden, to till the ground from which he was taken. He drove out the man; and at the east of the garden of Eden he placed the cherubim, and a sword flaming and turning to guard the way to the tree of life. (Genesis 3:23-24)

By juxtaposing "the devil's door" and the angels with their flaming swords, "The Iceman" creates mutually exclusive interpretive trajectories—is the couple driving to hell or to heaven? It is only in the song's last stanza that the confusion is, perhaps, clarified: "I say better than the glory roads of heaven, better off ridin' hellbound in the dirt." The angels are blocking the road to the town because, even though it is associated with hell, it is, in truth, the preferred destination.

"The Price You Pay" *(The River)*

Though the "The Price You Pay" was ultimately released on *The River*, it was one of six songs from that album slated to appear on *The Ties that Bind*, a 1979 studio album that was ultimately abandoned. I do not know when precisely it was composed, but the demos for the album were recorded in the first half of 1979 and *Darkness on the Edge of Town* was released in the summer of 1978, so it is not surprising to find thematic continuity between *Darkness* and some of the songs that followed it. The opening chords and forceful harmonica of "The Price You Pay" echo the opening of "The Promised Land" (discussed below) and the song builds on the critique of *Darkness on the Edge of Town*. The song opens with an image of a man driving through a desert highway, though the destination is the point where "you learn to sleep at night with the price you pay." The fate of the riders in the following stanzas is darker yet: they build roads to "ride to their death," they are trapped in a dream "where everything goes wrong," and the night's darkness "holds back the light of day." The fourth stanza alludes to the story of Moses and the Promised Land:

> Do you remember the story of the promised land
> How he crossed the desert sands
> And could not enter the chosen land
> On the banks of the river he stayed
> To face the price you pay

The critique resonates with the theological position of *Darkness on the Edge of Town*, refuting the notion that one can jump into a car and drive out to case the Promised Land. Noteworthy is the way Springsteen anchors this view in the biblical narrative, drawing on the fact that Moses lead the Israelites out of Egypt but never entered Canaan; he died on the eastern bank of the Jordan river.[9] In this, the sober tone of "The Price You Pay" is more faithful to the Bible than the facile Promised Land of *Born to Run*.

"Darkness on the Edge of Town" *(Darkness on the Edge of Town)*

The album's title track touches on all three of *Born to Run*'s redemptive elements. The opening line, "they're still racing out at the Trestles," informs us that *they* are still racing, but the singer no longer does. This assertion, on its own, leaves open the possibility that the singer has found another redemptive path. The phrase "that blood it never burned in her veins" suggests that a woman's disinterest in racing may have caused him to relinquish one redemptive path (the drive) for another (the woman). But this is not the case. The singer no longer maintains contact with the woman ("now I hear she's got a house up in Fairview"), nor even communicating with her directly—he instructs an unidentified interlocutor to relay a message to her ("tell her if she wants to see me..."). The song's nadir is the singer's matter-of-fact statement, "I lost my money and I lost my wife, them things don't seem to matter much to me now." Could the protagonists of "Thunder Road" or "Born to Run" refer to the loss of their love so coldly? Even the deeply flawed characters in *Born to Run*'s darker songs, "Jungleland" and "Meeting Across the River" are animated by love or at least by the hope for love. The singer in "Darkness on the Edge of Town," in contrast, is only willing to meet his former love once she has come to terms with the non-salvific darkness that surrounds

[9] Indeed, none of the adult Israelites who departed Egypt (except for Caleb and Joshua) cross into Canaan: "'As I live,' says the Lord, 'I will do to you the very things I heard you say. your dead bodies shall fall in this very wilderness ... not one of you shall come into the land in which I swore to settle you'" (Numbers 14:28-30).

them. For that is the sum total of his message: "Tell her, there's a darkness on the edge of town."

I noted at the end of the previous chapter that *Born to Run*'s power is largely centrifugal—the flight from the suffocating town toward a more authentic life elsewhere. Here, the singer points to a darkness that lies on the edge of town, meaning he is standing at the town's center. As the song reaches its conclusion, the singer takes a stand, proclaiming that "tonight I'll be on that hill 'cause I can't stop." Can't stop what? He cannot stop leaving the center of town and approaching its border, *without ever crossing it.* He does not plan to make an escape—there will be no flight to a better future; the farthest the singer is willing to venture is to the edge of town.

"Racing in the Street" *(Darkness on the Edge of Town)*

One of Springsteen's most haunting works, "Racing in the Street" opens with an extended ode to the singer's car, lovingly detailing its technical specifications: the year and make ('69 Chevy), engine type (396, a big block engine), the cylinder heads (fuelie), and the Hurst manual transmission. The singer and his partner, Sonny, built the car themselves and they drive it through the northeast racing circuits. In an ostensible sign of continuity with *Born to Run,* the singer describes racing as the marker of authentic living: some guys give up living and begin the slow, inexorable process of dying; others choose to "come home from work and wash up, and go racin' in the street." Racing, moreover, provides the singer with love, as he wins a woman's heart when he bests her then-boyfriend in a race. All the promises of *Born to Run* seem to have been fulfilled—the singer is suffused with a sense of authenticity, "Mary" has made the journey from the front porch to the front seat, and together they scream off into the night. But the truth is much darker; everything should be great, but nothing is. The singer's love cries herself to sleep, and is clearly depressed, as she sits alone in the darkness, staring "with the eyes of one who hates for just being born."

Why have things gone so wrong for a man who has lived in accordance with the promise of the salvific highway? This is precisely the point: things have failed *because* the singer has followed the logic of the open road, relegating the woman to the status of an accessory.[10] Consider her introduction in the song. Nestled between the singer's description of his car and his racing partner is the innocuous phrase "she's waiting tonight out in the parking lot, outside the 7-11 store." Crucially, the *she* waiting for him is the Chevy. Only much later do we discover that another *she* is waiting tonight—a woman staring into the darkness and sighing "baby did you make it all right?" The failure of the relationship is the failure of the racing narrative, since, as noted, they become a couple after the singer sees her "in a Camaro with this dude from L.A.," outraces the Camaro, and drives off with the girl, about whom we know nothing else. The singer describes his Chevy and his companionship with Sonny in greater detail than he does the woman he loves. In fact, we know more about her former boyfriend (a Camaro owner from Los Angeles) than about the woman. Is it any wonder she has fallen into depression? Where *Born to Run* aligns the car and the woman as compatible paths to this-worldly redemption, "Racing in the Street" suggests that they may be mutually exclusive. The singer says as much in the song's concluding lines:

> For all the shut-down strangers and hot-rod angels
> Rumbling through this promised land
> Tonight my baby and me we're gonna ride to the sea
> And wash these sins off our hands

Hot-rod angels rumbling through the promised land occupy the summit of *Born to Run*'s theology. But "Racing in the Street" pairs the hot-rod angels with shut-down strangers—an altogether apt description

---

[10] Springsteen recognizes that "Racing in the Street" breaks with earlier representations of the racing culture, though he suggests the relevant comparison is with the Beach Boys' "Don't' Worry Baby." "You put ten to fifteen years on the guy in 'Don't Worry Baby,' and he's the guy in 'Racing in the Street'," James Henke, "The Magician's Tools," *Backstreets* 89 (2010); reprinted in Phillips and Masur, *Talk About a Dream*, 403.

of the singer himself. Not the summit, then, but the nadir; the singer and his love will head out for a night drive no longer hoping for salvation, but rather for a chance to purge themselves of their sins.[11] And what, precisely, are the sins they need to wash off? The song does not mention infidelity, and the couple remains mutually committed. Even in her depressed state, the woman greets the singer's return home with care for his well-being. No, the sins are the actions that brought them to their current state: the immoderate love of the car; the belief that racing can be redemptive; the notion that relationships are decided by driving faster than a Camaro. The redemptive moments of *Born to Run* have become the sins of *Darkness on the Edge of Town.*

* * *

Thus far, I have argued that *Darkness on the Edge of Town* represents a methodic dismantling of the theological edifice Springsteen constructed in *Born to Run.* But the later album also offers a different theological paradigm in its stead, that of the apocalypse. *Apocalypse* is Greek for "revelation," but is used today in a narrower sense, referring to the revelations concerning the end of days, particularly the cataclysmic events preceding the endtime.[12] Thus, in the Hebrew Bible, a prophecy is revealed to Daniel that "there shall be a time of anguish, such as has never occurred since nations first came into existence. But at that time your people shall be delivered ... Many of those who sleep in the dust of the earth shall awake, some to everlasting life, and some to shame and everlasting contempt" (Daniel 12:1-2). Daniel does not understand the prophecy entrusted to him: "I heard but could not understand; so I said, 'My lord, what shall be the outcome of these things?'" (Daniel 12:8), but the heavenly figure transmitting the prophecy clarifies that Daniel

[11] The plural "our hands" suggests that the woman bears guilt as well—perhaps because she endorsed racing culture no less than the singer, driving off with him because he outraced her then boyfriend.

[12] For a helpful introduction to the topic see Martha Himmelfarb, *The Apocalypse: A Brief History* (Chichester, UK: Wiley-Blackwell, 2010).

does not need to understand it. "He said, 'Go your way, Daniel, for the words are to remain secret and sealed until the time of the end. Many shall be purified, cleansed, and refined, but the wicked shall continue to act wickedly. None of the wicked shall understand, but those who are wise shall understand'" (Daniel 12:9-13). The most important apocalyptic work, the New Testament book of Revelation tells of a vision communicated to John of Patmos, much of it devoted to a war that breaks out in heaven between the angels, led by the archangel Michael, and the dragon; terrible plagues visited upon the earth; the defeat of Satan; and the establishment of a new heaven and earth. Even from this very small sample of Daniel and Revelation passages, several related points may be gleaned. First, that both the time of the final revelation and the precise sequence of events leading up to it have already been established—the entire process is predetermined. Second, that the end of days will be accompanied by great violence. And finally, that the process does not allow for much in the way of human agency. Unlike the classical prophets of the Hebrew Bible, Daniel and John of Patmos are not instructed to preach repentance or social justice or proper worship to Israel and the Church, respectively. The actions of the believers neither engender the apocalyptic endtime, nor affect its course.[13] As we saw above, Daniel does not even need to understand the meaning of the message entrusted to him.

If so, *Darkness on the Edge of Town*'s denial of redemptive mobility is not only a critique of *Born to Run*, but also an important component in the formation of an apocalyptic subject—a person who discovers the world is indifferent to their hopes for salvation. Whether crashing their car into immovable objects or driving aimlessly, the characters on the album have been deprived of the possibility of transporting themselves from the one state of human existence to another, of escaping the fallenness into which they were born.

---

[13] The absence of human agency in apocalyptic works is a critical point of distinction between apocalypticism and prophecy. See John J. Collins, "Apocalyptic Eschatology in the Ancient World," in Jerry L. Walls, editor, *The Oxford Handbook of Eschatology* (Oxford and New York: Oxford University Press, 2008), 40-55.

"Badlands" *(Darkness on the Edge of Town)*

I began this chapter with the violence that opens "Badlands"—the nighttime trouble and the head-on collision, that together (I would now add) lead to a general feeling of helplessness: "I'm caught in a crossfire that I don't understand." The singer still has hope for a better, more authentic life, but he finds his efforts toward this end continually frustrated. Work, predictably, offers no reward. "Workin' in the fields, till you get your back burned, workin' 'neath the wheel, till you get your facts learned." The physical exertion is difficult, but more trying still is the lesson work imparts about the futility of believing that circumstances can meaningfully change. "Poor man wanna be rich; rich man wanna be king; and a king ain't satisfied till he rules everything." Ultimately, it does not matter if your work allows you to move from poor to rich or from rich to king—everyone is looking "up" at the people on the next level, holding tight to the lie that *they* live a blessed life. Even the king is haunted by the limits of his power, by his desire to rule everything, that is, to be a god.

Faced with the world's indifference, the best the singer can do is issue a series of hopeful calls to action, though he is not able to identify the requisite action or to specify how it will effect the desired change. The singer professes his faith—"I believe in the love that you gave me, I believe in the hope that can save me, I believe in the faith…"—alluding to Paul's first letter to the Corinthians: "And now faith, hope, and love abide, these three; and the greatest of these is love" (1 Corinthians 13:13).[14] But he has no way to translate this belief into action: "[I believe in the faith] and I pray that someday it may raise me above these badlands." *Someday it may* raise him up, but how and when this will happen remains unknown; he vows to "keep pushin' till it's understood and these badlands start treating us good," but how and when this will occur depends on forces beyond his control. The singer in "Thunder Road" urges Mary to join him because they have "one last

[14] On this reference, see Symynkywicz, *The Gospel According to Bruce Springsteen*, 46.

chance to make it real," but "Badlands" is no longer sure that this can be accomplished: "Talk about a dream, try to make it real; you wake up in the night, with a fear so real, you spend your life waiting for a moment that just won't come." True, the next line implores "don't waste your time waiting," but it is an empty exhortation that does not call to concrete action. The song never escapes the fear that all we can do is wait and hope for a redemptive moment that may or may not arrive. Not surprisingly, the simmering frustrations culminate in a cry for violence: "I wanna find one face that ain't lookin' through me, I wanna find one place, I wanna spit in the face of these badlands."

"The Promised Land" *(Darkness on the Edge of Town)*

"The Promised Land" opens "on a rattlesnake speedway in the Utah desert," far removed from the industrial northeast landscape of so many Springsteen songs, a location dictated by the song's theme, the Promised Land, and the singer's location in the unredeemed wilderness. In this desert existence, both work and the open road are bereft of meaning, as the singer spends his life "working all day in my daddy's garage; driving all night chasing some mirage."[15] Of course, the biblical desert wanderings are a temporary state and an integral part of the Israelite's Exodus from Egypt and journey to the Promised Land. In principle, then, the desert of "The Promised Land" might be a brief sojourn, a site of passage on the way to Canaan—but that is not the case:

> The dogs on main street howl,
> 'cause they understand,
> If I could take one moment into my hands
> Mister, I ain't a boy, no, I'm a man,
> And I believe in a promised land.

[15] On the desert motif, see Allen, "Puritan Ideal," 137: "In the songs 'The Promised Land' and 'The Price You Pay,' Springsteen sets his narratives in the middle of the desert, using the environment itself to invoke images of the Israelite wanderings in the wilderness." See also Arnoff (who does not refer to Allen), "A Covenant Reversed," 178-181.

The singer yearns to "take one moment," but cannot. He tries to affirm his manhood ("I ain't a boy, no I'm a man"), but instead undercuts it by addressing his interlocutor as "Mister," adopting the language of a boy, or a social inferior. He may want to ride "out *tonight* to case the promised land" (as in "Thunder Road"), but he has no access to it and so can only declare his faith in its existence: I believe in the promised land. The howling dogs—a classic cinematic harbinger of an approaching storm—highlight the external nature of the difficulties in *Darkness on the Edge of Town*. It is not enough to be inspired by the night or the road. There are tangible obstacles in the singer's way, and even the dogs can sense the imminent tempest. To his credit, the singer tries to overcome these obstacles. "I've done my best to live the right way, I get up every morning and go to work each day," but the world is indifferent to his efforts, and eventually his hope curdles, giving way to fantasies of violence—a homicidal explosion that will "tear this whole town apart," and a suicidal knife to "cut this pain from my heart."

The gathering pressure finally finds release in an apocalyptic storm. "There's a dark cloud rising from the desert floor, I packed my bags and I'm heading straight into the storm." Why would the dark cloud rise up from the desert floor rather than descend from the sky? The singer refers to the storm as a twister, but, meteorologically, twisters gather in the sky and then touch down (aside from the fact that they are atypical in Utah; most occur east of the Rockies). Biblically, however, the image resonates with Israel's desert wanderings on the way to the Promised Land: "The Lord went in front of them in a pillar of cloud by day, to lead them along the way" (Exodus 13:21).[16] The dark cloud invokes the biblical cloud, even as it stands in symbolic opposition to it insofar as the former will not lead the singer to the Promised Land. At this point, the singer recognizes that he has no other options: the car, the night, the woman, and now the cloud—none will lead him out of the desert. Knowing he is witnessing an apocalyptic force whose arrival heralds the imminent

[16] Ben Sommer suggests that the better biblical analogue is the storm at the end of Job, especially as the singer's drive "straight into the storm" echoes Job's demand that God speak to him from within the whirlwind. I believe the desert setting and explicit invocation of the Promised Land tilts the scales in favor of my interpretation, but Ben's argument is undoubtedly intriguing.

transformation of all reality—"a twister to blow everything down that ain't got the faith to stand its ground"—the singer rides into the storm.

The storm of "The Promised Land" is heir to the eschatological storms of the Bible, chief among them that of Revelation: "Then God's temple in heaven was opened, and the ark of his covenant was seen within his temple; and there were flashes of lightning, rumblings, peals of thunder, an earthquake, and heavy hail" (Revelation 11:19).[17] Like the storm in "The Promised Land," the biblical tempest is not a force of wanton destruction, but rather an event that distinguishes good from evil, the saved from the damned: "The sun shall be turned to darkness, and the moon to blood, before the great and terrible day of the Lord comes. *Then everyone who calls on the name of the Lord shall be saved*" (Joel 2:31-32). The storm, in other words, will destroy those who "don't have the faith to stand their ground." But the biblical precedent only gets us so far. The apocalyptic storms of the Hebrew Bible and the New Testament are, without exception, harbingers of a new reality. John of Patmos describes the transformation in cosmic terms: "Then I saw a new heaven and a new earth; for the first heaven and the first earth had passed away, and the sea was no more. And I saw the holy city, the new Jerusalem, coming down out of heaven from God, prepared as a bride adorned for her husband" (Revelation 21:1-2). But "The Promised Land," and *Darkness on the Edge of Town* as a whole, do not offer an account of the world that will arise after the destruction.[18] Also, the storm will not destroy a group whose evil behavior has doomed them to perdition, but rather "the dreams that tear you apart … the dreams that break your heart … the lies that leave you nothing but lost and broken hearted." Though manifested through the twister, the apocalyptic reckoning is internal, uprooting our dreams and the lies we tell each other and ourselves.

---

[17] See also: "Thus says the Lord of hosts: See, disaster is spreading from nation to nation, and a great tempest is stirring from the farthest parts of the earth!" (Jeremiah 25:32), and "Let all the inhabitants of the land tremble, for the day of the Lord is coming, it is near—a day of darkness and gloom, a day of clouds and thick darkness!" (Joel 1:1-2).

[18] The absence of a New Jerusalem, so to speak, from "The Promised Land" recalls the difference between "Lost in the Flood" and the Genesis flood story, discussed in chapter one. The biblical flood, for all its horror, laid the foundation for a new covenant between God and Noah; "Lost in the Flood" offered no vision of a better, postdiluvian, world.

What are these dreams and lies? On one level, these are the singer's promise that he is "gonna take charge" and his hope that he will "take one moment into [his] hand," when, in fact, he does not and, the song suggests, cannot. But in truth these are only the visible manifestations of the deeper lie of the Promised Land itself. For "The Promised Land" (the song) offers a systematic repudiation of the logic of the Promised Land (the concept), that is, of the salvific journey from fallenness to redemption. The singer remains lost in the desert, desperately maintaining his faith in a better future, though he has no clear path to it. This is why the song's reversal of the biblical desert cloud is so poignant: the meteorological phenomenon that ought to be leading him out of the desert (as it does the Israelites) instead announces his despair of the very idea of a redemptive journey. The singer can only drive into the storm—a gesture that is part flight, part suicide. This final act, a later iteration of Jimmy the Saint's ride into a hurricane in "Lost in the Flood," highlights the similarity between the two songs, with "Lost in the Flood" attacking traditional Christian teachings while "The Promised Land" attacks Springsteen's own earlier claims of the open highway. Like the sins of "Racing in the Street," the dreams and lies and twister comes to destroy are the salvific promises of *Born to Run*.

* * *

Theologically, Springsteen's albums up to *Darkness on the Edge of Town* constitute three distinct moments. The albums up to and including *Born to Run* contain a critical and a constructive argument: a critique of traditional religious symbols and institutions ("Lost in the Flood," "It's Hard to Be a Saint in the City," "If I Was the Priest"), alongside alternative, non-traditional moments of grace ("Does This Bus Stop at 82nd Street?" "Spirit in the Night") and worship ("Resurrection"). These culminate in *Born to Run*, which affirms the redemptive power of this world and holds it up as an alternative to traditional religion. "Thunder Road" acknowledges the power of Mary's religious worldview, but exhorts her to embrace the singer's vision of immanent redemption wrought through the salvific power of the night, the car, and romantic love ("Born to Run," "Night"). The theological elements in *Darkness on the Edge of Town* take up the earlier critique but redirect it toward the immanent theology of *Born to Run*, whose claims the later album deconstructs. However, it does not offer an alternate model of redemption, only a destructive vision of men powerless in the face of an indifferent world, and an imminent apocalypse.

Sin, Grace, and the Struggle Within

CHAPTER FOUR

Sin

A lot of the songs deal with my obsession with the idea of sin.[1]

The albums that follow *Darkness on the Edge of Town* do not form a clear theological trajectory. Accordingly, I no longer present the material in strict chronological order, instead devoting a chapter to each of the three theological topics that recur in Springsteen's post-*Darkness on the Edge of Town* writing: sin, redemption, and the struggle to embrace our better selves. I have tried to group together songs that address each topic in a similar manner, even if they appear on chronologically distant albums.

Sin, the subject of the present chapter, has already been discussed in the context of "Racing in the Street" where the singer and his love need to "wash these sins off our hands." As I noted in chapter three,

[1] Bruce Springsteen, discussing *Darkness on the Edge of Town*, in Zimny's *The Promise*, at the 59 minute mark.

this invocation of sin is unorthodox, as neither person has sinned in the conventional sense, but rather they have adopted a lifestyle that strains their relationship. I argue in what follows that, with one significant exception, this approach is typical of Springsteen's understanding of sin as the process by which decent individuals, confronted with difficult circumstances, lose touch with their better selves.

"Nebraska" *(Nebraska)*

The significant exception is the singer in "Nebraska," a song based on the Charles Starkweather and Caril Fugate murders. In December of 1957, Starkweather killed a gas station attendant, and a month later embarked on a killing spree, starting with Fugate's immediate family and followed by eight additional people over the subsequent two days. Starkweather was tried and executed in 1959, while Fugate was sentenced to life in prison, but secured her release in 1976. He was nineteen at the time, she fourteen. The singer recounts their first encounter in idyllic terms, "I saw her standin' on her front lawn just twirlin' her baton" but shifts abruptly to their crimes: "Me and her went for a ride sir and ten innocent people died." Now captured and awaiting execution, he is unrepentant, recounting the "fun" he had with his girl. In the concluding lines, the singer is asked to explain his actions and his answer is simply, "Well, sir, I guess there's just a meanness in this world." The response is plainspoken, as befits a twenty-year-old high school dropout, but nonetheless chilling. "Nebraska" does not try to explain the killer's actions in psychological terms (e.g., sociopathy), or refer to elements in his upbringing (e.g., abuse); his actions defy reduction to such terms. They are rather a manifestation of an evil, "a meanness," that exists in the world; a brute, irreducible fact.[2]

---

[2] As Irwin Streight has noted, the word "meanness" alludes to Flannery O'Connor's story "The River." See Streight, "The Ghost of Flannery O'Connor in the Songs of Bruce Springsteen," *Flannery O'Connor Review* 6 (2008), 13-14; and idem., "The Flannery O'Connor of American Rock," in Harde and Streight, *Reading the Boss*, 53-75. Springsteen has acknowledged O'Connor's influence on his writing: "At home, just before recording *Nebraska*, I was reading Flannery O'Connor. Her stories reminded me of the unknowability of God and contained a dark spiri-

Outside of "Nebraska," Springsteen's albums contain few unrepentant killers or irredeemably evil characters. More typical are the characters in the three songs to which I now turn, "My Father's House," "The New Timer," and "Devils & Dust"—fundamentally decent men who are beset by difficulties that have allowed the darker elements within them to dictate their actions.

"My Father's House" *(Nebraska)*

The phrase "my father's house" occurs in the Gospel of John, when Jesus exhorts his followers: "Believe in God, believe also in me. In my Father's house there are many dwelling-places. If it were not so, would I have told you that I go to prepare a place for you?" (John 14:1-2).[3] This is an enigmatic statement, not least to Jesus' disciples who press for a fuller explanation. Jesus replies with a series of affirmations concerning his unity with his father (or: Father): "No one comes to the Father except through me. If you know me, you will know my Father also" (John 14:6-7); "Whoever has seen me has seen the Father" (John 14:9); "Do you not believe that I am in the Father and the Father is in me? The words that I say to you I do not speak on my own; but the Father who dwells in me does his works. Believe me that I am in the Father and the Father is in me" (John 14:10-11). Jesus insists that he and his father are inextricably interconnected, and additionally that his father's house is sufficiently large to welcome many under its roof. John 14:2 is also the inspiration for the gospel song "In My Father's House," that was recorded by the Blackwood Brothers in 1954, but gained greater prominence when Elvis Presley covered it on his first gospel album, *His Hand in Mine* (RCA Victor, 1960). The song refers to the father's toil on behalf of his son ("he's preparing me a mansion there"), and emphasizes the inclusive

---

tuality that resonated with my own feelings at the time," Bruce Springsteen, *Songs* (New York: HarperEntertainment, 2003), 136.

[3] The phrase also occurs in the Gospel of John's account of the expulsion of the money changers from the temple. Finding the court filled with "people selling cattle, sheep, and doves, and the money-changers seated at their tables" (John 2:14), Jesus cries out: "Take these things out of here! Stop making my Father's house a market-place!" (John 2:16).

nature of the promise since it is open to anyone who acts righteously ("if you're true then to this land you'll surely go").

Springsteen's "My Father's House" opens with a dream. The singer, as a young boy, rushes through the forest, trying to reach his father's house before darkness falls. The world outside the protective confines of the house is threatening, diabolical: "I heard the wind rustling through the trees and ghostly voices rose from the fields," with "the devil snappin' at my heels." Ultimately, the boy is able to break into a clearing where he sees his father's house "shining hard and bright," and he runs to the comfort of his father's arms. The dream's light-darkness symbolism is conventional. The thickening darkness gives rise to demonic threats, while the house's illumination marks it as a site of both physical safety and paternal love. Dreaming of his childhood home, the singer's imagery resonates with the Blackwood Brothers' characterization of the brightness of the heavenly city, "[my father] has gone away to live in that bright city," and "soon there'll come a bright tomorrow, when the world will all be free from sin and strife." In both the earlier song and in the dream sequence of "My Father's House," light stands for the possibility of a father's embrace, whether earthly or divine.

Awakening to find himself surrounded by darkness—the physical darkness of night and the symbolic darkness of separation from his father—the singer reflects on "the hard things that pulled us apart," vowing to set things right with his father. He rises, dresses, and drives off; as he approaches the house "I could see its windows shining in light," the house's illumination slicing through the darkness, beckoning the son to return to his father.[4] At this point, both the singer and the listener have every expectation that the son and father will be reunited. But when the singer reaches the house, an unfamiliar woman answers the door and informs him that his father had long ago moved from that house and she has no information as to his whereabouts. The singer, then, is not at his father's house at all, and it is not clear that he ever will be. The woman's words, spoken with both kindness and caution from behind

[4] The darkness of the family home is a symbol of father-son estrangement in "Independence Day" (*The River*) as well, where "the darkness of this house has got the best of us."

the chained door, accentuate the loss: "I'm sorry *son*, but no one by that name lives here anymore." The singer had come to the house in the hope of repairing his relationship with his father, but he will only be addressed as *son* by a stranger. The song concludes with a harsh transformation:

My father's house shines hard and bright
It stands like a beacon calling me in the night
Calling and calling so cold and alone
Shining 'cross this dark highway where our sins lie un-atoned

The light of the father's house continues to shine, but the light symbolism has been upended so that the illumination now serves as a beacon reminding the son of his unatoned sins. But what are these sins? The song speaks only of "the hard things that pulled us apart," presumably some combination of external circumstances and internal family dynamic, but the failure to overcome these obstacles is, for Springsteen, a form of sin. The house that in the Gospel of John symbolized the intimate bond between the son and the father and the promise of future acceptance, is here a cold monument to the loss of past intimacy and the failed attempt to recapture it.[5]

"The New Timer" *(The Ghost of Tom Joad)*

The New Timer is a man who falls on hard times and begins to work as a migrant laborer, traveling across the United States from one temporary job to the next. In his travels, he meets Frank, the old timer to the singer's new. Frank shows the singer kindness, helping him navigate a difficult new reality and offering an optimistic, live-and-let-live philosophy: "You don't cross nobody, you'll be all right out here, kid." But Frank's words are harrowingly disproved. After the two part ways, the singer receives word that Frank was brutally murdered, killed for no reason in an act of

[5] "Wages of Sin," a *Born in the U.S.A.* outtake released on *Tracks*, contains a similar dream sequence to "My Father's House," but there the sin is the mistrust and abuse a romantic couple inflict on one another.

gratuitous violence. The news of Frank's senseless death devastates the singer, who begins to reminisce about the home he left behind, but he does not return to his family, and the song ends with the New Timer huddled by a campsite, clutching a machete, steeped in hatred:

> My Jesus, your gracious love and mercy
> Tonight I'm sorry could not fill my heart
> Like one good rifle
> And the name of who I ought to kill

Despite the horror of the situation, the confession is surprisingly tender. The New Timer addresses Jesus directly, humbly acknowledging Christ's gracious love and mercy even as he laments their insufficiency. The old timer had shown the singer earthly love and mercy in his time of need, and his murder has so shaken the singer that Jesus cannot quell his desire for revenge.[6] The singer does not rail against Jesus for allowing such crimes to occur, but rather offers his own spiritual shortcomings as an apology of sorts. Jesus, after all, explicitly rejects killing as a punishment for murder. Invoking Exodus 21:23-24 ("life for life, an eye for an eye, a tooth for a tooth"), he says, "You have heard that it was said, 'An eye for an eye and a tooth for a tooth.' But I say to you, Do not resist an evildoer. But if anyone strikes you on the right cheek, turn the other also" (Matthew 5:38); similarly, "Love your enemies and pray for those who persecute you, so that you may be children of your Father in heaven; for he makes his sun rise on the evil and on the good, and sends rain on the righteous and on the unrighteous" (Matthew 5:44-45). The New Timer cannot live up to the New Testament's teachings concerning enemies, and this is the sin he repents to Jesus.[7]

---

[6] According to Symynkywicz, the singer "lies in bed with a machete close at hand and prays to Jesus to feel hope and faith and love again, but these graces never arrive" (*The Gospel According to Bruce Springsteen*, 128). But this description grossly understates the darkness of the song. The New Timer is not praying to Jesus for spiritual rehabilitation; he is confessing that divine grace is incapable of displacing his desire for revenge. For other examples of Symynkywicz's overly sunny interpretations, see the discussion below, chapter six, n. 28.

[7] It is noteworthy that the song recounts a "traditional" sin as well, Frank's murder, but Springsteen is uninterested in that crime, focusing instead on the New Timer's failure to be his best self.

"Devils & Dust" *(Devils & Dust)*

The singer of "Devils & Dust" is a soldier who finds himself in a war far home—Iraq, given the timeframe of the song's composition and release—addressing a fellow soldier named Bobbie. The song consists of the singer's thoughts about his task as a soldier, human nature, and the cost of war. He is in evident distress, as he speaks of an inability to know whom to trust and the troubling distance from home. But in later stanzas he shifts to a different register, affirming people's fundamental goodness, their shared desire to "find the love that God wills and the faith that He commands," and invoking God as witness to the justice of his cause ("I got God on my side and I'm just trying to survive"). Nonetheless, he comes to recognize that, irrespective his view that the inclination of the human heart is toward good, under certain circumstances the heart will turn: "fear … [will] take your God filled soul and fill it with devils and dust." Conversion from God to the Devil does not require sinful behavior or the adoption of illicit theological doctrines. It suffices to find oneself far from home, surrounded by fear and moral ambiguity. The most significant biblical reference is found in a dream narrative in the third stanza:

> Well I dreamed of you last night, Bobbie
> In a field of mud and bone
> Your blood began to dry
> And the smell began to rise

As Matthew Orel has noted, the singer's dream is a reversal of Ezekiel's vision of the Valley of the Dry Bones, in which God sets Ezekiel in the middle of a valley full of dry bones and instructs the prophet to foretell their resurrection.[8] Ezekiel does so, and

> suddenly there was a noise, a rattling, and the bones came together, bone to its bone. I looked, and there were sinews on

[8] Matthew Orel, "From Adam to Jesus: Springsteen's Use of Scripture," 145.

> them, and flesh had come upon them, and skin had covered them; but there was no breath in them. Then he said to me, 'Prophesy to the breath, prophesy, mortal, and say to the breath: Thus says the Lord God: Come from the four winds, O breath, and breathe upon these slain, that they may live.' I prophesied as he commanded me, and the breath came into them, and they lived, and stood on their feet, a vast multitude. (Ezekiel 37:7-10)

Instead, Orel argues, "'Devils & Dust" turns Ezekiel's vision on its head. The dream is of dry bones, but they are not revived, for "[w]hat rises from the bones isn't living people but a smell—a smell of death."[9] In this sense, the dream emphasizes the desperation of the singer's predicament: where Ezekiel prophesies life, the soldier is haunted by death.

There is a second, more subtle dynamic at work, whose meaning derives from the political and theological context of Ezekiel's vision. Ezekiel is a prophet of exile, part of the Judean community living "by the rivers of Babylon" (Psalm 137:1) following the Babylonian emperor Nebuchadnezzar's destruction of Jerusalem. The historical and geographic setting is important first and foremost because Babylonia is modern-day Iraq. The soldier in "Devils & Dust," then, is located at the site of Ezekiel's vision, the shared location highlighting the difference between the singer and the biblical prophet. Ezekiel's vision is political. It is addressed to a community of Israelites exiled to Babylon in the wake of a military defeat, and holds the promise of national renewal. Though the exiles' fate looks grim at present, a better future awaits—the dead bones will live once more, and the currently vanquished will be shown to be the true victors. The content of the prophecy confirms the universal power of Israel's God, who promises redemption to the exiled people. In setting forth this vision, Ezekiel also endorses a theological universalism already implicit in the fact that he continues to prophesy even though he is in a state of exile, standing on foreign soil. The revolutionary force of Ezekiel's prophecy should not be overlooked. Broadly speaking, Ancient

---

[9] Orel, "From Adam to Jesus," 145.

Near Eastern cultures linked the political fate of a religious collective with the power of its deity: a vanquished nation was tantamount to a vanquished national god. How, then, could the universal God also be the national God of a defeated nation?[10] Ezekiel's vision of the valley of the dry bones affirms God's universal sovereignty both in its vision of Israel's future revival, and in its communication on Babylonian soil.

"Devils & Dust" offers the opposite vision. Politically, Ezekiel's Israelites are the exiled victim of an invading empire, while the singer is part of an invading empire; the Israelites are vanquished but will, in time, regain their power, the singer and his comrades enter Iraq/Babylon as the most powerful military force in the world, yet will not long enjoy the status of victors. Where Ezekiel's vision foresees resurrection, the singer's dream sees only death. The song's theology similarly contravenes Ezekiel's. Where the prophet speaks of God's continued heed for a vanquished nation, the singer claims that "God is on my side," a triumphalist return to the theology that pits a nation's god against the god of its enemies, identifying military victory with divine endorsement.[11] The singer stands where Ezekiel once stood, but the imperial ambitions and nationalist theology he embodies identify him as the political and theological heir to Babylon, not Israel. And therein lies sin.

"I'll Work for Your Love" *(Magic)*

"I'll Work for Your Love" is about a different type of sin. As in "My Father's House," the sin involves the way the song's characters treat one

[10] The prophet Isaiah faced the same question when the northern kingdom of Israel was destroyed by the Assyrians in 721 BCE, and he resolved the tension by casting the military victors as unwitting pawns in God's plan: "Ah, Assyria, the rod of my anger—the club in their hands is my fury! Against a godless nation I send him, and against the people of my wrath I command him, to take spoil and seize plunder, and to tread them down like the mire of the streets" (Isaiah 10:5-6). The "godless people" in question are the Israelites who failed to worship God properly, and the Assyrian invasion is Israel's punishment for this transgression. While it appears to the outside viewers that Israel (and, by extension, the God of Israel) has been vanquished, in fact Assyria is an unsuspecting pawn in God's hand, the instrument by which God punishes Israel for its misdeeds.

[11] The more immediate precedent to the singer's affirmation that God sides with him is Bob Dylan's anti-war song "With God On Our Side," from *The Times They Are A-Changin'* (Columbia, 1964). The basic message of Dylan's song is that *everyone* thinks God is on their side.

another, but its commission involves more than allowing outside forces to tear the relationship apart, and it elicits correspondingly greater guilt and contrition. The song opens with the juxtaposition of domestic and biblical imagery, the intimate setting of a couple in their kitchen as the man requests a drink: "Pour me a drink Theresa in one of those glasses you dust off." But the second half of his sentence —"and I'll watch the bones in your back like the stations of the cross"—shatters the domestic mood, abruptly introducing an analogy between Theresa's back and Jesus' final journey through the Via Dolorosa ("The Way of Suffering") to his crucifixion and entombment. The Stations of the Cross evoke Christ's betrayal, his physical agony, and his death in atonement for the sins of mankind. It would be a gross understatement to characterize this image as unromantic, and its juxtaposition with the couple's kitchen conversation is perplexing. The next line further likens Theresa to Jesus in the Passion Narrative: "Round your hair the sun lifts a halo, at your lips a crown of thorns." The halo is a standard element in the iconographic representation of holiness, but the symbolism of the crown of thorns is much darker. The crown, along with the scarlet robe (scarlet being the Roman color of royalty), is used by the Roman soldiers to mock the claim that Jesus is King of the Jews: "Then the soldiers … stripped [Jesus] and put a scarlet robe on him, and after twisting some thorns into a crown, they put it on his head. They put a reed in his right hand and knelt before him and mocked him, saying, 'Hail, King of the Jews!'" (Matthew 27:27-29). Why is this imagery associated with Theresa? The last line of the stanza clarifies the dynamic between the couple: "Whatever the deal's goin' down, to this one I'm sworn, I'll work for you love." The singer does not know how the situation will be resolved, but affirms his willingness to work for Theresa's love. The first stanza does not yield a clear picture, but Theresa's association with the iconography of Christ's suffering is suggestive of betrayal.

The second and third stanzas confirm this interpretation, as the singer describes a loss that has befallen the couple, and affirms his determination to salvage whatever he can of their love. The most explicit allusion to the nature of the crisis occurs in the third stanza: "Now I see … our book of faith's been tossed." The husband and wife were joint authors of a book of faith, presumably a shared life based on trust, that has now been lost. This loss of faith has a devastating effect on the couple, as "the pages of Revelation lie open in your empty eyes of blue." Revelation, the last book of the New Testament, recounts the apocalyptic travails of the end of days, evoking the possibility of the end of the couple's shared days.[12] The imagery of a crisis that is at once religious and marital finds its fullest expression in the subsequent line: "well tears they fill the rosary, at your feet my temple of bones, here in this perdition we go on and on." The rosary is both a series of prayers recited in contemplation of the mysteries of Jesus' and Mary's lives, and the string of beads that guide the supplicant through the correct prayer sequence. Whether the song intends the former (tears are shed during the recitation of the rosary) or the latter (tears physically fall on the prayer beads), the man is praying and weeping simultaneously. The "temple of bones" is likely his body, so the image is heartbreaking: the singer lies at Theresa's feet, crying for the losses they have suffered, and perhaps for his role in the loss, while praying that she will allow him to work for her love.

The end of the song offers a moment of hope, when "in the late afternoon, sun fills the room with a mist in the garden before the fall." The line can be interpreted as either seasonal or scriptural. On the former understanding, the late summer sun creates a mist in the couple's garden before the arrival of autumn (*fall* refers to the season); on the latter, "in the garden before the fall" alludes to the blessed condition of Adam and Eve in the Garden of Eden before sin (*fall* refers to the fall of man). The warm sun and the allusion to a time before sin suggest a moment of grace, perhaps renewed hope for the couple, but it is short-lived. "I watch your hands smooth the front of your blouse and seven drops of blood fall." The seven drops recall either the tradition that Jesus' blood was shed seven times, or the seven sorrows of Mary.[13] The return to the garden does not last, and the song concludes with these drops of blood, symbols of betrayal and suffering, the marital sin refracted through the biblical.

---

[12] On the book of Revelation, see the discussion above, chapter three.

[13] The seven sorrows of Mary form a popular Catholic devotion based on tribulations Mary endured throughout her life, beginning with the prophecy spoken by Simeon when the infant Jesus was presented at the Jerusalem Temple (Luke 2:34-35), through placing Jesus' body in a tomb (John 19:40-42).

"Reason to Believe" *(Nebraska)*

Like the title track of *Nebraska*, "Reason to Believe" is a theological outlier from *Nebraska*, though it is not concerned with the sins of one man, but rather with the sins of humanity. The song, often cited as the uplifting conclusion to *Nebraska*, consists of four stanzas. In the first, the singer sees a man standing on the side of the road, his car door flung open, struggling to come to terms with death of a dog he presumably just hit. The driver is so confounded by the situation, so incapable of accepting the dog's death, that he stands there for some time, poking the dog with a stick, "like if he stood there long enough that dog'd get up and run." This response strikes the singer as "kinda funny," and the stanza concludes with the broader observation that "at the end of every hard-earned day, people find some reason to believe."

The second stanza describes loss of a different sort. Mary Lou loved Johnny and was devoted to him, promising to bring her earnings home to support him. Yet, despite Mary Lou's best efforts, one day Johnny leaves her for no apparent reason. Mary Lou, like the driver poking the dead dog, cannot reconcile herself to the loss, "and ever since that, she waits down at the end of that dirt road for young Johnny to come back." Again, the singer notes, the situation "struck me kinda funny," but affirms that, ultimately, people find a reason to believe.

The third stanza is a brief portrait of the cycle of human existence: a baby is born, named ("Kyle"), and baptized in the river; an old man dies, is buried, and his body prayed over. The singer does not find anything "funny" about this, and instead turns to God and pleads, "Lord won't you tell us, tell us what does it mean? At the end of every hard-earned day, people find some reason to believe." The question is interesting for its shift to a first person plural ("tell *us* what does it mean"), presumably a reference to humanity as a whole. It is not clear what in the third stanza elicits the statement about people finding some reason to believe. Is this merely the chorus, repeated mechanically between two stanzas, or does the affirmation respond to the description of baby's birth and the man's death?

The fourth stanza conforms to the pattern established in the first two. A congregation gathers to celebrate a wedding, but the bride never arrives; long after the guests have dispersed, the groom stands alone, gazing at the river and "wonderin' where can his baby be." The song ends with a final assertion that "still, at the end of every hard-earned day, people find some reason to believe."

The song undoubtedly affirms humanity's capacity to believe, a point some scholars interpret as uplifting, as when Irwin Streight writes that "this final song seeks to resolve the litanies of meanness, desperation, hopelessness, and longing recounted in the preceding stories, and to resolve them in a decidedly Catholic fashion."[14] However, this reading is not congruent with the way belief functions in the first, second, and fourth stanzas. The driver lingering over the dead dog, Mary Lou waiting at the end of a dirt road, the groom wondering "where can his baby be" though it is clear to all she is no longer "his baby"—all three clutch at a belief because they cannot come to terms with a loss.[15] Their belief is not anchored in reality: there will be no canine resurrection, and it is almost as certain that young Johnny and the runaway bride are never returning. If so, the refrain that "people find some reason to believe" is not an optimistic affirmation, but rather a melancholy truth about people's ability to maintain belief in the face of loss, despite overwhelming evidence to the contrary and their our own best interests. After all, the protagonists of these tales would be better served by *abandoning* their belief and moving on as best they can.

---

[14] Streight, "The Ghost of Flannery O'Connor," 15.

[15] Streight has argued that the song "concludes with a picture of a groom standing waiting for his bride, even after all the congregation is gone–the classic image in Christian eschatology for the expectation of Christ's return to claim *His* bride, the Church" ("The Ghost of Flannery O'Connor," 15; emphasis in the original). The jilted groom, in other words, is an allegorical representation of the church awaiting the return of Christ. One obvious difficulty with this interpretation is that it gets the gender symbolism wrong: Christ is the groom whose return is awaited, while in the song it is the bride who departs. At a minimum, then, this is not "the classic image of Christian eschatology." Moreover, the song's bride abandons the groom with no indication that she will return—a poor analogue to the promised Second Coming of Christ. Most problematic is Streight's isolated invocation of allegory. It would be one thing if he claimed that "Reason to Believe" is an allegorical composition, and provided a compelling interpretation of the song as a whole (the driver, the dog, Mary Lou and Johnny, and so on); but one cannot cherry-pick a single line in a song and characterize it alone as allegorical.

The third stanza is more difficult to interpret since it does not portray an individual incapable of coming to grips with loss, but it nonetheless contains several clues. One is the song's broader context: the first, second, and fourth stanzas all portray belief as a coping mechanism that in some cases borders on delusion. It is possible, therefore, that the third stanza's message is, similarly, that the people placing infant Kyle in the river because the waters wash away his sins, and those praying over the body of a man who died impoverished and apparently alone—they too are deluding themselves. This interpretation is buttressed by the singer's cry "Lord, won't you tell us, tell us what does it mean?" and the silence it elicits. As I noted above, the first-person plural pronoun gives the question a universal force, mankind turning to God in a plea for meaning. A baby's birth, and old man's death—what does it mean? This is the most explicitly religious line in the song, and it may be the darkest as well, as it dispenses with the pretext that God might answer, and moves immediately to the familiar statement about people's belief. On this interpretation, the cry "Lord won't you tell us … what does it mean" invokes a twofold absence: the absence of any apparent meaning to human existence, which motivates the cry, and the absence of God, who does not respond to it. If so, the plea to God is another indication of our inability to confront absence (of ultimate meaning to human existence, as well as of God), and to relinquish belief even when we would be better off doing so. According to this interpretation, "Reason to Believe" makes the most troubling claim of all—that belief itself can be a sin.[16]

---

[16] The critique of belief as an impediment to action can already be found, in an attenuated form, in *Darkness on the Edge of Town*. The singer in "Badlands" affirms "I believe in the faith that can save me, I believe in the hope and I pray that someday it will raise me above these badlands," yet he remains as much a prisoner of his unredeemed life as several of the characters on *Nebraska*. Similarly, the singer in "The Promised Land" repeatedly confesses his belief in the Promised Land, but he never even journeys toward it, much less finds it, instead driving into an apocalyptic storm. What good, then, are these professions of belief? See also Dave Marsh's comment that the song "stared straight into the void about which Springsteen-as-Starkweather spoke and found there exactly what was expected: nothing at all," Dave Marsh, *Glory Days: The Bruce Springsteen Story* (New York: Thunder Mouth's Press, 1996), 123.

CHAPTER FIVE

Grace and Redemption

I could never get that redemption stuff out of my work or out of myself; it's there to stay[1]

In a 2006 interview with Phil Sutcliffe, Bruce Springsteen discusses what it means to lead a spiritual life that refuses any claims to absolute truth. It is "a life of mystery" that embraces our own uncertainty, our own inability to provide answers to every question, even while remaining attentive to the blessings in our midst. "We live in a tragic world, but there's grace all around you. That's tangible. So you try to attend to the grace." Sutcliffe presses Springsteen to clarify what he means by that word, and he elaborates: "Grace to me, it's just the events of the day. The living breath of our lives … So you're chauffeuring your kids somewhere and you think it's a burden and something happens … it's there."[2] This very

[1] Springsteen in a benefit for *Double Take* magazine, February 19th, 2003; cited in Dinerstein, "The Soul Roots," 458, n. 53.

[2] Phil Sutcliffe, "You Talkin' To Me?" *Mojo* (UK) 146, January 2006, 76 – 98; reprinted in Phillips and Masur, *Talk About a Dream*, 319.

personal statement succinctly captures the dominant tone in Springsteen's later characterization of grace as an immanent event, a redemptive experience embedded in the lived reality of everyday life. The lion's share of this chapter examines the various realms Springsteen, post-*Darkness on the Edge of Town*, identifies as sources of grace and redemption.

"Youngstown" *(The Ghost of Tom Joad)*

As I noted in chapter three, though *Darkness on the Edge of Town* critiques many aspects of *Born to Run*, in both albums work is devoid of meaning and often oppressive. The experience of the worker in "Night" waking up to the sound of the factory bell and surviving the boss's abuses from nine to five is essentially the same as that of the man raging against his daily work in "Badlands," or of the workers in "Factory." "Youngstown," in contrast, is literally a love song to the steel mills of northeast Ohio. The chorus, "my sweet Jenny I'm sinkin' down, here darlin' in Youngstown," is not addressed to a woman, but rather to "Jenny," the blast furnace that powered the Brier Hill plant of the Youngstown Sheet and Tube Company, named for Mary Jeannette Thomas, the daughter of the owner of the steel company.[3] The singer serenades Jenny as he would a lover.

Much of "Youngstown" recounts the earlier relationship between the mills and the workers, a relationship based on shared service to the nation. The mills produced the armaments that supplied the Union, and later the American army in its foreign wars. The workers, for their part, served in the military in World War Two, Vietnam, and Korea. Most importantly, the mills sustained the local community, but like much of *The Ghost of Tom Joad*, "Youngstown" chronicles the decline and eventual demise of one aspect of the American Dream, namely, the blue-collar worker who can provide for his or her family with dignity. The mills' owners betray the community, and the country as a whole turns its back on the workers, who are left to reconsider their sacrifices on the battlefield, "wondering what they were dyin' for." But the unraveling of the mill-workers' social

---

[3] See Sherry Lee Linkon and John Russo, *Steeltown U.S.A.: Work and Memory in Youngstown* (Lawrence, KS: University Press of Kansas, 2002), 24.

contract only highlights the importance of the work that sustained their families and community, and the song characterizes the mills in openly salvific terms, with "them smokestacks reachin' like the arms of God, into a beautiful sky of soot and clay." This simile represents a marked break with the traditional topography of divine revelation. Instead of descending from up high, in "Youngstown," the divine smokestacks rise up from the mill and into the sky. God's presence is here, on earth, not in heaven.

A second theological reversal follows. After outlining the decline of his beloved town and industry, the singer concludes with an unusual wish:

> When I die I don't want no part of heaven
> I would not do heaven's work well
> I pray the devil comes and takes me
> To stand in the fiery furnaces of hell

There is a long tradition of poets preferring hell to heaven, going back at least as far as Immanuel of Rome (1261-1328), an early Renaissance Hebrew poet:

> Deep in my heart I have resolved to
> spurn the garden of Eden in favor of
> Hell, for there I shall find dripping
> honey and nectar: all the graceful does
> and lustful ladies.
> [...]
> Hell, I consider you excellent in charm
> and grandeur, for you house all the
> girls in their elegant dresses. It is you
> who have assembled all the delights of
> our eyes.[4]

---

[4] Immanuel of Rome, "Eden and Hell," in *The Penguin Book of Hebrew Verse*, edited and translated by T. Carmi (New York: Viking Press and Penguin Books, 1981), 421-22.

Immanuel accepts the notion that heaven is intended for the good and hell for the bad—he simply prefers the company of the bad. Immanuel's view is typical. Mark Twain is said to have quipped "heaven for climate; hell for the company";[5] Pearl Dickson, in "Little Rock Blues," prefers Little Rock to heaven, "I started to heaven; but I changed my mind, I'm going to Little Rock; where I can have a better time";[6] and Billy Joel would "rather laugh with the sinners than cry with the saints, the sinners are much more fun."[7] The singer in "Youngstown," in contrast, does not identify with hell because of its lustful ladies or fun-loving sinners, but rather because Hell is where he can continue to ply his trade.[8] This last claim involves yet another theological reversal, of the symbolic meaning of fire.

The theological tradition associates fire with hell and God's judgment. The Hebrew prophet Malachi teaches that divine wrath destroys by fire: "See, the day is coming, burning like an oven, when all the arrogant and all evildoers will be stubble; the day that comes shall burn them up, says the Lord of hosts, so that it will leave them neither root nor branch" (Malachi 4:1). In the New Testament, Jesus speaks of the coming of the Son of Man in similar terms: "Then he will say to those at his left hand, 'You that are accursed, depart from me into the eternal fire prepared for the devil and his angels'" (Matthew 25:41).[9] In medieval iconography, too, fire is the dominant image of hell. "Youngstown" turns this tradition on its head. So devoted is the singer to the steel mill's furnaces, that he prefers to spend all eternity in the fires of hell than ascend to heaven.

Two points concerning this last statement merit mention. First, the song judges the world-to-come by the standards of earthly reality,

---

[5] See *When in Doubt, Tell the Truth: And Other Quotations from Mark Twain*, edited by Brian Collins (New York: Columbia University Press, 1997), 62.

[6] Reed, *Holy Profane*, 57.

[7] Billy Joel, "Only the Good Die Young," on *The Stranger* (Columbia, 1977). There is a tradition, perhaps apocryphal, that on his deathbed Niccolo Machiavelli said that he preferred the company of the great Pagan philosophers in hell to the Christian saints in heaven.

[8] It is worth noting how far removed the singer of "Youngstown" is from the other Springsteen character who prefers hell to heaven—"The Iceman": "better than the glory roads of heaven, better off ridin' hellbound in the dirt." See the discussion in chapter three, above.

[9] See also, Luke 16:23-24 and Revelation 20:10.

indeed by the standards of daily labor. The singer does not dispute the association of hell and fire; he simply holds that the positive work of the mill's furnaces outweighs the traditional assessment, transforming hellfire from a form of damnation to a desired setting for the afterlife. This shift is analogous to the image of "smokestacks reachin' like the arms of God, into a beautiful sky of soot and clay" in its insistence that the lower, earthly reality determines the divine, not vice versa. Second, the singer never entertains the possibility that the afterlife is a place of leisure. He asks only, Where am I more suited to work? Where can I be more productive? Since the singer believes that he "would not do heaven's work well," the priority of hell over heaven becomes self-evident. Though the conclusion of the song is a bit tongue-in-cheek (the singer is not seriously hoping to spend eternity in hell), it highlights the profound transformation of work relative to Springsteen's early albums, as "Youngstown" identifies it as the path to salvation—in this world and in the next.

"Leap of Faith" *(Lucky Town)*

The claim that sexual pleasure is analogous to religious ecstasy is a well-worn trope in popular music, more often presupposed than developed.[10] Occasionally, however, songwriters offer more robust explorations of the theme, as in "Holy Ghost," a 1979 single by the Bar-Kay's, a Stax recording group that started out as Otis Redding's band: "Girl, your love is like the Holy Ghost, shakin' all in my bones … Girl, your love is like the Holy Ghost, I feel like I've been born a second time."[11] More recently, Bruno Mars's "Locked Out of Heaven" describes the singer's sexual relationship with a woman as a full-fledged religious experience: "You bring me to my knees, you make me testify … I'm born again each time you spend the night."[12] Springsteen explored this motif early on in "When You Dance," a

---

[10] Springsteen's strong and vocal support of gay rights notwithstanding, his poetic representation of desire is heteronormative, and my analysis is largely determined by Springsteen's lyrical choices. My discussion (and, I trust, Springsteen's lyrics) applies to the love and desire experienced by all, irrespective sexual orientation.

[11] "Holy Ghost" was released by the Bar-Kays on *Money Talks* (Stax, 1978); see the discussion in Reed, *Holy Profane*, 31.

[12] Bruno Mars, *Unorthodox Jukebox* (Atlantic, 2012).

song that he performed beginning in 1970: "And when you love, our love shakes the heavens above."[13] He revisits the redemptive power of physical intimacy in a more sustained manner in "Leap of Faith."

The song opens darkly, with rain pouring all over the world and the singer lamenting that "heartbreak and despair got nothing but boring," presumably because they have been his companions for some time. The tone brightens significantly when a woman enters his life, and the chorus proclaims the importance of a leap of faith, of overcoming heartbreak and remaining open to the possibility of new love. The phrase "leap of faith" normally refers to the insufficiency of rational thought in the search for ultimate religious truths, an idea that can be traced at least as far back as Tertullian, the second and third-century Church Father who asserted that his belief in the tenets of orthodox Christianity was grounded in, rather than challenged by, their absurdity.[14] Several important theologians (Martin Luther most prominent among them) formulated similar critiques of philosophy, and the of broader assumption that human reason offers the best path toward understanding the world, characterizing this view as a type of intellectual hubris.[15] In its modern manifestation, the leap of faith is most closely associated with the thought of the Danish philosopher Søren Kierkegaard, who refers to the inadequacy of reason and the need to leap *into* faith.[16] The faith Springsteen extols, however, is not religious, but rather romantic. A cerebral approach to romance can lead to endless deliberation and doubt; no one can prove to us that it is better to remain hopeful in the face of the real possibility of pain and heartbreak. It takes a leap of faith.

---

[13] "When You Dance" was recorded by Southside Johnny and the Asbury Jukes on *This Time It's For Real* (Epic, 1977), but the recording is of a later version of the song that does not contain the lyrics cited above.

[14] For an accessible survey see Pierre Bühler, "Tertullian: The Teacher of the *credo quia absurdum*," in Jon Stewart, editor, *Kierkegaard and the Patristic and Medieval Traditions* (Burlington, VT: Ashgate, 2008), 131-142.

[15] Luther's claim that reason is "the devil's whore" is characteristic of a significant stream in his writings, but does not do justice to the complexity of his views. For a concise discussion see Colin Brown, *Christianity and Western Thought: A History of Philosophers, Ideas, and Movements* (3 vols; Downers Grove, IL: InterVarsity, 1990), 1.148-51.

[16] For a survey of key thinkers grappling with this issue see C. Stephen Evan, *Faith Beyond Reason: A Kierkegaardian Account* (Grand Rapids, MI: Eerdmans, 1998), and the discussion of Kierkegaard at 78-92.

The song's second stanza enumerates some of the earthly rewards that accrue to the leaper, as Springsteen playfully conflates the divine and the carnal: "Now your legs were heaven, your breasts were the altar, your body was the holy land." The analogies are frankly sexual, and the identification of the woman's body with the holy land particularly ribald, as the desert wanderings end by entering the holy land. But, surprisingly, the entrance is deferred. After surveying his lover's body and singing its praises, the singer recounts, "You said 'jump' but my heart faltered, you laughed and said 'Baby don't you understand?' It takes a leap of faith…" The faltering heart is curious, as the song has thus far been uninterested in the emotional dimension of this relationship, focusing instead on the woman's body as the site of erotic desire. Moreover, the next stanza maintains the erotic focus, describing the couple's sexual union. Overcoming the "faltering," then, resulted in intercourse, and not (or not primarily) in emotional intimacy. While I recognize that this interpretation is speculative, it is possible, in light of the unambiguously sexual content of the song, that "my heart faltered" is a euphemism for a (temporary) sexual shortcoming on the singer's part.

Whatever the precise nature of the faltering, the singer overcomes it and the relationship is consummated, when "you were the Red Sea, I was Moses, I kissed you and slipped into a bed of roses, the waters parted and love rushed inside." In this brilliant and hilarious metaphor, Springsteen likens the singer's libidinal success to Moses standing at the Red Sea—the biblical parting of the waters an analogue to the woman welcoming a lover into her body. Indeed, Springsteen's sexual interpretation can be pressed further once we consider God's precise instructions to Moses, who is standing by the Red Sea as Pharaoh's army draws near: "Then the Lord said to Moses, 'Why do you cry out to me? Tell the Israelites to go forward. But you raise up your rod …'" (Exodus 14:15-16).[17] The sea only opens once the rod is raised.[18]

[17] For a psychoanalytically oriented reading of the symbolism of Moses' rod in Exodus see Ilona N. Rashkow, "Oedipus Wrecks: Moses and God's Rod," in Timothy K Beal and David M. Gunn, editors, *Reading Bibles, Writing Bodies: Identity and the Book* (London and New York: Routledge, 1997), 72-84.

[18] As it happens, this is not the only sexual Moses allusion in Springsteen's corpus. "Red-Headed Woman" is a celebration of the joys of a redheaded lover, replete with graphic descriptions of the singer's desire for the woman and their sexual activity. At the end of *The Ghost of Tom Joad* acoustic tour, Springsteen added a new line—"well push comes to shove and shove comes to push, and

The Moses allusion, it should be noted, is not only sexual. The parting of the Red Sea occurs at a critical juncture in Israel's journey out of the slavery of Egypt and toward the Promised Land, when their situation—trapped between the Red Sea and Pharaoh's army—appears hopeless. Moses, however, does not lose faith and continues to follow God's instructions, and ultimately the sea yields, affording the Israelites safe passage. Translated into the song's register, the story of the parting of the Red Sea is an admonition not to lose hope even in dire straits; to be willing to take a leap of faith.

At this point we find the most perplexing line of the song and one of the most obscure biblical references in Springsteen's writings. After celebrating his romantic and sexual renewal, the singer asserts, "I was Jesus' son sanctified." Let me confess at the outset that I have not found a compelling interpretation of this phrase.[19] If we take it as a direct reference to Jesus, it represents an interesting twist on the Gospel account of Jesus' virgin birth.[20] "I was Jesus' son sanctified" imagines that Jesus himself sired a son, a child whose birth would be institutionally illicit, since Jesus was never married nor, for that matter, did he enter into a sexual relationship.[21] Such a birth would also upset deeply held assumptions about the early church and its generally negative view of sexuality. Had Jesus sired a son (who freely identified himself as Jesus'

I was Moses kneeling 'fore the burning bush"—a play on the dual signification of kneeling (pious and sexual), and the raunchy double entendre of "bush."

[19] Most commentators pass over this statement in silence: Orel, "From Adam to Jesus," 152, discusses "Leap of Faith" but not Jesus' son; Symynkywicz, *The Gospel According to Bruce Springsteen*, 110, writes "Springsteen pronounces himself 'sanctified' by the whole experience," but does not mention the phrase "like Jesus' son."

[20] There is fairly broad scholarly consensus that the doctrine of the Virgin Birth was not current among the earliest followers of Jesus. The Gospel of Mark (widely held to be the earliest of the gospels) does not mention it, and there are tensions within and between the infancy narratives that do. Moreover, neither Paul (the earliest of the New Testament authors) nor any of the gospel traditions attributed to Jesus refer to Jesus being born of a virgin. See the classic presentation of the problem by Raymond E. Brown, *The Virginal Conception and Bodily Resurrection of Jesus* (New York: Paulist Press, 1973), 21-68. As always, the relevant context for my analysis is Christian traditions as they came to be understood by later generations, not their historical accuracy.

[21] In keeping with the previous comment, my concern here is with the representation of Gospel figures in the Catholic Church, and need not address the historical questions raised by the recent discovery of a papyrus attributing the words "my wife" to Jesus. On this find see Karen L. King, "'Jesus Said to Them, "My Wife ..."': A New Coptic Papyrus Fragment," *Harvard Theological Review* 107 (2014), 131-59.

offspring), a wholesale revision of some core beliefs regarding the value of sexual abstinence would be called for. Yet the singer speaks of himself as Jesus' son who is *sanctified through sex.*[22]

The song's conclusion returns to the redemptive power of the new relationship. The rainfall associated in the opening line with "heartbreak and despair" is transformed into "sweet blessings rain[ing]" down on the couple, a phrase drawn from an early twentieth century hymn named "Showers, Sweet Showers," that still retains the religious overtones of its original context. The singer tells his lover he can sense the first breeze of summer, that is, that the rains that were falling in the opening of "Leap of Faith" have passed. The passing of the rains echoes the Song of Songs, where the end of the rainy season marks the beginning of love: "Arise, my love, my fair one, and come away, for now the rainy season is past, the rain is over and gone" (Song of Songs 2:10-11). The allusion to the Song of Songs is particularly apropos since this dialogue between lovers is arguably the most explicitly sexual book in the Hebrew Bible, replete with erotic imagery, as when the woman calls out, "Awake, O north wind, and come, O south wind! Blow upon my garden that its fragrance may be wafted abroad. Let my beloved come to his garden, and eat its choicest fruits" (4:16). The man responds, "I come to my garden, my sister, my bride; I gather my myrrh with my spice, I eat my honeycomb with my honey, I drink my wine with my milk" (5:1). A few verses later

[22] I do not have sufficient confidence in this interpretation to include it in the body of the book, but I want to acknowledge the possibility that "Jesus' son" alludes to Lou Reed's song "Heroin," from The Velvet Underground's album *The Velvet Underground and Nico* (Verve, 1967). The song is a first-person narrative, a rambling account of the experience of a heroin addict, including the line "things aren't quite the same, when I'm rushing on my run, and I feel like Jesus' son." The juxtaposition of Springsteen and Lou Reed may appear forced, but Springsteen was close to New York's punk scene during the 1970's. He collaborated with Patti Smith on "Because the Night" and wrote "Hungry Heart" for the Ramones, though Jon Landau, Springsteen's manager, prevailed upon him to record it himself. Springsteen even made a brief cameo Lou Reed's *Street Hassle* (Arista, 1978). Speaking of Springsteen's guest vocals, Reed recalls, "I was there, Bruce Springsteen was there, Patti Smith was there" (Chris Roberts, *Lou Reed: Walk on the Wild Side* [Milwaukee, WI: Hal Leonard, 2004], 88). The "Heroin" reference is fairly obscure, and many years elapsed between the two albums, but if "Leap of Faith" does allude to Lou Reed's lyrics, it suggests that entering into a sexually intimate relationship with a woman is akin to the high of the heroin addict, though a high that is "sanctified." See Springsteen's comments on working with Reed in Dave DiMartino, "Bruce Springsteen Takes It to the River," *Creem* (January, 1981); reprinted in Burger, *Springsteen on Springsteen*, 120. The connection between "Jesus' son" and Lou Reed is noted by Kirkpatrick, *Magic in the Night*, 164.

the woman describes the effects of the man's visit: "My beloved thrust his hand into the opening, and my inmost being yearned for him. I arose to open to my beloved, and my hands dripped with myrrh, my fingers with liquid myrrh, upon the handles of the bolt" (Song of Songs 5:4-5). By alluding to this biblical poem, "Leap of Faith" identifies itself as part of a literary tradition reaching back to the Hebrew Bible, that celebrates both the physical and spiritual significance of sex. The song concludes with a final religious image: "in your love I'm born again."

"Human Touch" *(Human Touch)*

"Human Touch" revisits the themes and arguments of "Thunder Road," with the singer delivering an extended monologue to woo a woman and exhorting her to avoid applying religious ideals to human relationships in an attempt to avoid life's complexity and risk. The song's opening sets the tone: "Girl ain't no kindness in the face of strangers, ain't gonna find no miracles here."[23] The *here* in question is not a particular location, but rather the world itself that is devoid of divine grace, "a world without pity," and it is an error to expect gifts from above: "Ain't no bread from heavenly skies, ain't nobody drawin' wine from this blood." The first statement invokes the Manna, the bread that God provided for the Children of Israel as they journeyed through the desert,[24] while the second appears to allude to Jesus' instruction that his disciples drink from a cup of wine "for this is my blood" (Matthew 26:28).[25] In fact, "Human Touch" reverses the New Testament account, as Jesus speaks of wine being transformed into blood, while the song speaks of blood that could (but will not) be will not be transformed into wine, a reversal motivated by the need to align the miracles such that both yield unearned sustenance. This is scripturally true of the Manna, food provided by the grace of God ("Manna from heaven" still

[23] This sentiment is echoed in "The Long Goodbye," also from *Human Touch*: "Waitin' on rain, hangin' on for love; words of forgiveness from some God above. Ain't no words of mercy comin' from on high, oh no, just a long goodbye."

[24] The Manna episode occurs in Exodus 16:1-36.

[25] On these verses, see the discussion of "Lost in the Flood" in chapter one.

refers to an unearned gift), but Springsteen must reverse the wine-into-blood transformation so that it too signifies the miraculous (and thus unearned) production of a drink.

Like Mary in "Thunder Road," the woman in "Human Touch" still holds out hope for an ideal relationship, but the singer responds that "you can wait on your blessings my darlin', but I got a deal for you right here." The woman has experienced pain and heartbreak and now seeks security, but the "feeling of safety you prize, well it comes with a hard, hard price." Here the song's theological and the romantic claims coalesce. The absence of divine grace and miracles forces us to confront the fact that we will not be provided for by others. But despite the similarities to "Thunder Road," the later song's insistence that "it's just you and me tonight" is not cause for celebration, and the vision of romantic love in "Human Touch" is greatly diminished; it does not claim to offer redemption beneath the hood of a car or know the way to the Promised Land. The singer does not lure her with salvific promises, instead acknowledging the woman's fears, even as he notes—"you been broken and you been hurt, show me somebody who ain't." The car too is stripped of its redemptive promise, becoming a vehicle of self-effacement. "Yeah I know I ain't nobody's bargain, but hell a little touchup and a little paint..." The statement trails off in a guarded ellipsis, but the meaning is clear—the singer is like a dinged up car that might, with a little work (though hopefully not a major overhaul), still prove serviceable. Absent an alternate redemption narrative, the singer's modest hopes are for companionship in daily life: "I just want someone to talk to," and "I just want to feel you in my arms." But he worries that even this scaled-back aspiration overreaches. "Tell me, in a world without pity, do you think what I'm askin' too much?" Like his predecessor in "Thunder Road," the singer in "Human Touch" rejects the promise of other-worldly intervention, and extends his hand to a woman, but he recognizes that even the modest desire for a woman's company, for someone to talk to and hold in his arms, may be more than this world allows.

"My Beautiful Reward" *(Lucky Town)* and "Happy" *(Tracks)*

A similar, if slightly more optimistic picture emerges from "My Beautiful Reward" and "Happy," two versions of the same song. In "My Beautiful Reward," the singer recounts the different paths he traveled searching for a beautiful reward, including riches and "my own drug to ease the pain," as well as encounters of a more spiritual nature: "From a house on a hill a sacred light shines; I walk through these rooms but none of them are mine." The first half of this densely allusive line recalls Jesus' teaching at the Sermon on the Mount: "You are the light of the world. A city built on a hill cannot be hidden. No one after lighting a lamp puts it under the bushel basket, but on the lampstand, and it gives light to all in the house" (Matthew 5:14-15). The house bathed in sacred light thus serves as an image of religious salvation. The second half of the line recalls the verse "in my Father's house there are many dwelling-places" (John 14:1), but the singer does not recognize any of the house's rooms as his own and continues on his search.[26] Interestingly, the rejection of heavenly salvation does not pave the way for an earthly counterpart. The singer experiences love that leads to heartbreak and the song ends in a dreamlike scene. Transformed into a great black bird, he soars through the night sky, still "searching for my beautiful reward."

"Happy," a version of the song that was recorded for *Lucky Town* but released on *Tracks*, charts a different course. Its opening lines are almost identical to "My Beautiful Reward," but the first-person narrative of the latter ("I sought gold and diamond rings") is replaced with a third-person account ("Some need gold and some need diamond rings"). "Happy" also adds to the list of failed paths the "promise of a better world to come, when whatever here is done," that is, the religious promise of an afterlife. But the singer wants none of it, as his happiness is found in his lover's arms.[27] He returns to the inadequacy of transcendent comfort

[26] See the discussion of "My Father's House" in the previous chapter.

[27] The word "happy" can denote a fleeting feeling of pleasure or contentment. Here it likely, though not definitely, means something closer to "blessed," as it does in the standard translation of a number of biblical passages, most famously Psalm 1:1 ("Happy are those who do not follow the advice of the wicked").

when, in the next stanza, he speaks of a house on "a distant hill" where the laughter of children rings and guardian angels watch from above, though their presence cannot assuage the singer's fears, as "at night I feel the darkness near." His only consolation is his love's physical presence: "I awake, I find you near."

Human existence, according to "Happy" is generally short and troubled, with men and women "[circling] each other in a cage" in a wary mating ritual. But there is an egress from these limitations, albeit a temporary one: "Tonight let's shed our skins and slip these bars, happy in each other's arms." The couple's loving embrace allows them to transcend the physical ("skin") and societal ("bars") limitations of the human condition. The claim is plainly paradoxical. How can the couple transcend physicality through physical intimacy? How can they shed their skin by lying in each other's arms? But here, as elsewhere, Springsteen insists that the transformative power of love is irreducibly physical; a transcendence *within* the realm of the physical, not beyond it. The lover's body plays a dual role, as both a physical safe haven in an oft-hostile world, and as the site of love's transcending power.

"Kingdom of Days" and "This Life" *(Working on a Dream)*

The idea that salvific grace can be recovered from the quotidian reality of our lives expresses itself with particular clarity in a pair of songs from *Working on a Dream*, that together constitute Springsteen's meditations on the meaning of love in the face of the vastness of time and space.

Time is perhaps the starkest line of demarcation between the human realm and the divine. The passage of time suffuses every aspect of our world, from the passage of the seasons, through the grand arc of history, to the trajectory of each individual life. But time has no dominion in the divine world.[28] The division between the temporality of human

[28] Whether this means that God exists within time but is without beginning and end, or that God stands outside time altogether, is a matter of debate. For a defense of the idea that God exists separately from time (rather than at all moments in time), see Paul Helm, *Eternal God: A Study of God Without Time* (Oxford: Clarendon, 1988); for a recent survey of the various arguments, see William Lane Craig, *Time and Eternity: Exploring God's Relationship to Time* (Wheaton, Il: Crossway, 2001).

existence and the eternity of the divine is already noted in the Bible. The Psalmist writes, "before the mountains were brought forth, or ever you had formed the earth and the world, from everlasting to everlasting you are God" (Psalm 90:2), and Isaiah speaks of God as "the high and lofty one who inhabits eternity" (Isaiah 57:15); the New Testament Epistle to the Hebrews addresses God as eternal creator, for "in the beginning, Lord, you founded the earth, and the heavens are the work of your hands; they will perish, but you remain; they will all wear out like clothing; like a cloak you will roll them up, and like clothing they will be changed. But you are the same, and your years will never end" (Hebrews 1:10-12). Later thinkers built on this biblical foundation, establishing temporality as the constitutive distinction between the human and the divine. St. Augustine devotes Book 11 of the *Confessions* to time and eternity, emphasizing the unbridgeable gap between the two and hence between humanity and God: "Your years neither come nor go … your years are one day, and your day is not each day, but today … With you, today is eternity."[29] Among Jewish authors, one of the most moving poetic representations of this divide is the liturgical poem "Let Us Affirm the Holiness of the Day" (*U'ntaneh Tokef)*, that highlights the ephemeral nature of human existence:

> For they are flesh and blood
> Their origin is from dust
> And their end is to dust
> […]
> Like a passing shadow and like a vanishing cloud
> And like blowing wind and like swirling dust
> And like a passing dream
> But You are king, the living and everlasting God
> Your years are boundless and the length of your days endless.[30]

---

[29] *The Confessions of Saint Augustine* 11.15, translated by John K. Ryan (New York: Doubleday, 1988), 252.

[30] The translation (with minor changes) is by Joel M. Hoffman, in Lawrence A. Hoffman, editor, *Who By Fire, Who By Water: U'ntaneh Tokef* (Woodstock, VT: Jewish Lights, 2010), 31-32. This liturgical poem is the inspiration for Leonard Cohen's "Who By Fire."

"Kingdom of Days" is permeated with the passage of time, as the singer watches the sun rise and set, traces the path of the moon in the sky, and feels the change of seasons. But the temporal nature of his life is tempered by love, for in the presence of his lover he does not "hear the minutes ticking by" or "feel the hours as they fly"; he knows time is passing, yet feels as though it has stood still. However, love's transformative power is not reducible to psychological terms, since it somehow does transcend time: "When I count my blessings and you're mine for always, we laugh beneath the covers and count the wrinkles and the grays." The line is knowingly paradoxical. The singer is well aware that he and his lover are growing old, as they count their wrinkles and gray hairs, yet he insists that she is his "for always"—the very opposite of mortality. Clearly the singer is not referring to metaphysical eternity, but rather to an "always" he claims for finite creatures such as ourselves. Though the broader environment—the natural world, the cycle of human life—is ineluctably temporal, the singer identifies a region of "always" nestled within it, and so reverses the traditional theological hierarchy: the eternal does not transcend the earthly by being outside or beyond it, but rather by creating a separate reality that is still earthly, an *always* that exists within finitude.[31]

Two intertextual references stress the theological force of "Kingdom of Days."[32] The phrase "when I count my blessings" alludes to the famous gospel hymn "Count Your Blessings," that urges us to "count your blessings, name them one by one, count your blessings, see what God hath done" and so recognize that true blessings are our "reward in heaven [and] home on high."[33] But the singer in "Kingdom of Days" *has* counted his blessings and finds that the chief among them is his love's presence by his side, in the here and now. The second intertextual reference is the song's title, an allusion to the biblical concept of the

[31] Speaking of this song, Springsteen notes that "there seems to be a transcendence of time in love." See Mark Hagen, "Meet the New Boss," *The Guardian* (January 17, 2009); reprinted in Phillips and Masur, *Talk About a Dream*, 361.

[32] By "intertextual" I mean a reference to or invocation of an earlier text that helps shape the meaning of the current one. The earlier text is sometimes referred to as the intertext.

[33] The hymn was composed by Johnson Oatman Jr. (1856-1922).

kingdom of God (or the Kingdom of Heaven), perhaps most famously expressed in the verses that would come to be known as the Lord's Prayer: "Our Father in heaven, hallowed be your name. Your kingdom come. Your will be done, on earth as it is in heaven" (Matthew 6:9-10). The phrase "kingdom of days" neither affirms nor denies the kingdom of God, but rather insists on the reality of "*our* kingdom," a kingdom that at once consists of and transcends the passing days. The song is permeated with minor daily moments, visual and tactile impressions of the couple's shared life: "My jacket 'round your shoulders, the falling leave, the wet grass on our back as the autumn breeze drifts through the trees." From these quotidian elements, transformed by love, the singer constructs his kingdom of days.

"Kingdom of Days" describes love's power to transform eternity into the singer's lived experience. "This Life" makes a similar claim in terms of space, albeit in less explicitly theological language. The song begins by juxtaposing cosmic events of incomprehensible magnitude with the experience of a man standing by the woman he loves, seeing the birth of the universe and the staggering amount of time elapsed since then reflected in her eyes: "a bang then stardust in your eyes, a billion years for just this night." The singer studies the emptiness of the universe with his telescope, "searching for a home," but knows that the vast reaches of the cosmos are aloof to human needs. We may yearn to physically transcend our terrestrial existence, but to no avail, "we reach for starlight all night long, but gravity is too strong, chained to this earth we go on and on and on…" The song's chorus replays the tension between transcendence and immanence. "This life, this life and the next, with you I have been blessed, what more can you expect?" The concept of the next life typically denotes a religious existence subsequent to death, but in the same breath the chorus anchors the singer firmly in this world, as blessedness comes not from divine grace but rather from being with his love, the very pinnacle of blessedness—"what more can you expect?" The song ultimately resolves the tension between the apathy of the cosmos and the meaning the singer finds in his love's eyes. The universe will remain vast and aloof, but his love is *his* universe: "I finger the hem of your dress, my universe at rest."

"Living Proof" *(Lucky Town)*

Like "Kingdom of Days" and "This Life," "Living Proof" identifies a realm of transcendence within a world that the song characterizes as otherwise dirty, foul and confused. The song unfolds as a classic conversion narrative. The singer was once lost, having abandoned his true identity and given up his faith in himself, "tryin' to shed my skin … to burn out every trace of who I'd been." Predictably, he falls into a state of wretchedness, doing sad and hurtful things, trapped in a prison of his own making. Redemption comes not from above, but from the love of a woman who can see past the rage, and helps the singer emerge from his self-imposed incarceration.

This woman bears the singer a son, an event described as "a little piece of the Lord's undying light," and "the missing words to some prayer"; proof of God's mercy. Despite the religious language, this transformative event does not transport the singer to a different reality. The birth of his child creates a transcendent sphere within this world that, notably, underscores the fragility of the singer's life:

> Well now all that's sure on the boulevard
> Is that life is just a house of cards
> As fragile as each and every breath
> Of this boy sleepin' in our bed

The song's final verse, "[we will] steal what we can from the treasures of the Lord," recalls casing the Promised Land in "Thunder Road."[34] The religious redemption the song offers the couple is not given freely from above—it is up to them to steal it, and, with the birth of their son, they have. But "Living Proof" does not share the bravado of "Thunder Road." The singer is not a winner breaking out of a town

[34] I owe this insight to John Rak (personal communication).

full of losers; he is a man transformed by fatherhood, fiercely alive to the transcendent joy of his son's birth, but also aware of the terrifying fragility that accompanies it.

"Hunter of Invisible Game" *(High Hopes)*

"Hunter of Invisible Game" weaves together two narrative threads, one a series of biblically allusive scenes of the singer preparing for foreboding, even apocalyptic events. The first stanza has the singer pulling himself from a ditch to build "an ark of gopher wood and pitch," a clear allusion to Noah's ark, which God commanded Noah to make "of gopher wood … and cover it inside and out with pitch" (Genesis 6:14). But as of the stanza's conclusion, the flood has not come and the singer is left sitting by the roadside and waiting for the rain to fall. The second stanza finds the singer awakening to the sound of trains and the sight of a scarecrow on fire and "empty cities and burnin' plains,"[35] a phrase that recalls the destruction of Sodom and Gomorrah, when "the Lord rained on Sodom and Gomorrah sulfur and fire" (Genesis 19:24), while Abraham "looked down towards Sodom and Gomorrah and towards all the land of the plain, and saw the smoke of the land going up like the smoke of a furnace" (Genesis 19:28). The anticipation of destruction by flood and the judgment executed upon the burning cities instill a sense of dread, though the singer is never present when the violence occurs. He then travels with unnamed companions through a bone yard, along a path of black smoke, to "the valley, where the beast has his throne"—presumably in preparation for an apocalyptic battle, preparations still ongoing when the stanza ends: "I sing my song and I sharpen my blade." All is in readiness, but the battle does not commence. As in the first stanza, the singer readies himself, but the event does not (yet?) materialize. Perhaps this is the

[35] I cannot identify the motif of the burning scarecrow with certainty. "Scarecrow on Fire" is the title of a very beautiful poem by Dean Young, published in his collection *Fall Higher* (Port Townsend, WA: Copper Canyon, 2011), 9. Young's poem does not relate directly to the images in the second stanza of "Hunter of Invisible Game" and the poem's relevance to the song remains speculative.

meaning of the phrase "invisible game"—the singer is a hunter that never confronts his prey.

The second narrative thread considers the physical reality of a lover's presence, contrasting it with the distance and perhaps irreality of the grand biblical themes:

> Strength is vanity and time is illusion
> I feel you breathin', the rest is confusion
> Your skin touches mine, what else to explain
> I am the hunter of invisible game

Within the swirl of biblical imagery and the promise of momentous change triggered by cleansing floods and ultimate battles against evil, the singer finds solace—he finds *reality*—in the touch of his lover's skin and the sound of her breath. Warring theological and political claims fade before the irreducible truth of her presence. "Through the empires of dust, I chant your name," the ephemeral existence of the empires a foil to the constancy of his lover and of his calls to her.[36] The last stanza appears to pick up the first thread, exhorting the listener to prepare for "the hour of deliverance" when "high hope and faith and courage" will be tested. In fact, the song is not concerned with the religious end of days, but rather with what it has all along indicated is ultimately real: "There's a kingdom of love waiting to be reclaimed."

"We Are Alive" *(Wrecking Ball)*

"We Are Alive," another song filled with dark biblical imagery but an ultimately hopeful message, opens with a reference to biblical resurrection—"there's a cross up yonder on Calvary Hill," the site of

[36] There is an intimation of this view in the opening lines of "I Wanna Be With You," which was recorded for both *Darkness on the Edge of Town* and *The River* but released on *Tracks*: "Let the frozen cities crumble, crumble and fall, that's alright, I don't mind at all, let 'em all tumble right into the sea … I wanna be with you." As though the woman's presence so totally eclipses all else, that the singer is untroubled by the collapse of entire cities.

Jesus' crucifixion. But as the song unfolds, we learn that the singer is telling a young man about the nightly resurrection that occurs nearby. "There's a graveyard, kid, down below, where at night the dead come to life," though they are not physically resurrected; the bodies remain alone in the dark as the spirits rise up.

The implicit division between the mortal body and immortal soul might be taken as an allusion to traditional Christian doctrine, but the voices rising from the grave teach otherwise. One was killed in Maryland in 1877, in the Great Train Strike; another, on a Sunday morning in 1963 Birmingham, presumably in the bombing of the 16th Street Baptist Church; a third while crossing the southern desert in search of a better future for children left behind. These individuals gained eternal life by dying for a greater cause—fair labor, civil rights, the well-being of their children—thereby transcending death. This remains their motivation after death, "to carry the fire and light the spark, to stand shoulder to shoulder and heart to heart," to continue the struggle they waged in their lifetimes. The singer then describes his own death:

> Well I awoke last night in the dark and dreamy deep
> From my head to my feet my body'd gone stone cold
> There were worms crawling all around me
> My fingers scratchin' at an earth black and six foot low

The imagery of a worm-infested corpse scratching to get out of the earth, a tableau that recalls Hieronymus Bosch, highlights the ultimate fate of the body in the solitude of the grave. But the singer's initial fear of an eternity in solitude is allayed when he hears the voices rising up around him, proclaiming "we are alive!" The religious ideal of resurrection is at once affirmed and reimagined as living on after death through the good we contributed to our families and our communities in the course of our lives.

"Rocky Ground" *(Wrecking Ball)*

"Rocky Ground" mobilizes an array of biblical motifs to describe a deeply flawed reality, and promises imminent (but not immanent) redemption. The singer and his community have been "traveling over rocky ground," and have faltered; they must pay the price of their sins before redemption is possible: "Before we cross that river wide, the blood on our hands will come back on us twice." This language echoes the rebukes of the ancient prophets, as when Isaiah chastises Israel, saying "your iniquities have been barriers between you and your God, your hands are defiled with blood" (Isaiah 59:2). But unlike Isaiah, the singer is himself part of the sinning congregation, a lost man who prays his best is good enough, raises his children to do right, and hopes throughout for divine assistance or even a sign, but none is forthcoming. "Where you once had faith," he concedes, "now there's only doubt; You pray for guidance, only silence now meets your prayers; The morning breaks, you awake, but no one's there."

But while the world is without divine presence, the singer assures us that change is coming in the form of a great purification that harks back to the biblical purges: "Forty days and nights of rain washed this land; Jesus said the money changers, in this temple will not stand." Just as the great biblical flood cleansed the land of sin and paved the way for a new beginning; just as Jesus expelled the money changers from the Jerusalem Temple, seeking to restore the institution to its intended sanctity,[37] now a storm is gathering and it is time to lead the flock to higher ground. Protected from the deluge, they will make their way to Canaan.

The allusion to the biblical flood (that also lasted forty days and forty nights) offers an interesting comparison with Springsteen's use of the flood motif in his earlier work. As I argued in chapter one, in "Lost in the Flood," the deluge is not redemptive, but rather part of the fallen reality that greets the Gunner's return: "Have you thrown your senses to

[37] Though often portrayed as a break with Temple Judaism, Jesus clearly seeks to reform the institution and restore its original glory. "Then Jesus entered the temple and drove out all who were selling and buying in the temple, and he overturned the tables of the money-changers and the seats of those who sold doves. He said to them, 'It is written, "My house shall be called a house of prayer"; but you are making it a den of robbers'" (Matthew 21:12-13).

the war or did you lose them in the flood?" Indeed, "Lost in the Flood" traces the singer's inexorable corruption, as the warnings he issues the Gunner and the kid in Jimmy the Saint's wreckage give way to his casual abandonment of a wounded man "holding his leg screaming something in Spanish, still breathing when I walked away." The singer in "Rocky Ground," in contrast, welcomes the purifying flood: he is one of those who will survive its ravages and inherit a better world. As he jubilantly cries toward the end of the song, "A new day's coming!"

"Heaven's Wall" and "This Is Your Sword" *(High Hopes)*

In these songs, both from his latest album, Springsteen employs relatively straightforward biblical allusions in the service of a communal ideal, creating songs whose language and themes would not be out of place in a traditional hymnal. "Heaven's Wall" opens with a young woman drawing water from a desert well while speaking of Jesus' (or God's) ability to restore sight to the blind and raise the dead.[38] In the song's concluding stanza, the singer enumerates instances of God's providential care—looking over the watcher at the gates, Jonah in the belly of the whale, and *you* (either an addressee in the song or the listener) in times of distress, and all the while "His mercy did not fail." Between these stanzas, the singer exhorts the "men of Gideon," the "men of Saul," and the "sons of Abraham" to raise their hands "and together we'll walk into Canaan land."

The entry into Canaan is closely associated with entry into heaven—the song's characters are located outside heaven's wall—and the common theme with some of Springsteen's earlier works highlights how dramatically his poetic vocabulary has changed. For one, earlier songs described an individual or a couple attempting to enter the Promised Land, as in "The Promised Land" and "Thunder Road," respectively. "Heaven's Wall," exhorts a collective. More accurately, it exhorts three biblical collectives: "men of Gideon" invokes the biblical judge (or chieftain) who led the

[38] The woman uses the pronoun "he" without specifying the identity of the referent.

Israelites against the Midianites (Judges chapters 6-8); "men of Saul" invokes the followers of the first Israelite king; and "sons of Abraham" is a broader genealogical-religious group of Abraham's descendants. Another point of difference, "Heaven's Wall" is not interested in the journey to the Promised Land, that is, in the salvific transition from an unredeemed state to redemption; its concern is the moment of entry into Canaan.

"This Is Your Sword" issues a similar battle cry, as the singer bequeaths a righteous weapon, "this sword of our fathers," and a protective shield to his brothers and sisters. The sword and shield are necessary to ward off the darkness all around, the despair that can cause one to grow callous and apathetic, to "close your mind and empty your heart." But to do so is to lose sight of the God-given beauty that fills the world, and of the promise of future miracles. When we "stare into the abyss" we may be overcome by despair, and must arm ourselves with the only antidote, love. "This is your sword, this is your shield; this is the power of love revealed." The notion of redemptive love marks a return of sorts to the worldview of *Born to Run*. But "This Is Your Sword" does not endorse romantic love and its protagonists are not a couple; this is the love a community bestows on its members.

"Mary's Place" *(The Rising)*

In "Living Rock 'n' Roll," an unreleased song dating to the Steel Mill/ Child[39] period mentioned briefly in chapter one, Springsteen describes rock 'n' roll as a conversion experience: "Mama, mama, won't you come and see, see what the music has done to me, gone all through my fingers, gone down deep into my soul." The song's second and fifth stanzas characterize music as the earthly heir to the traditional role of religion, "a revelation" that "gives my life a real salvation." "Mary's Place" revisits this idea, but where the earlier song described music displacing traditional religion, "Mary's Place" offers a more complex picture.

The song opens with a series of ecumenical images—seven pictures of Buddha, the prophet, and eleven angels of mercy. The mood is somber,

[39] Child was Bruce Springsteen's band during 1969, prior to being renamed Steel Mill.

as the angels are sighing over some dark, unidentified event the singer refers to as "that black hole in the sun." His heart too is dark, though it is "rising," trying to overcome the darkness. The next line is something of a paradox: "I'm pullin' all the faith I can see from that black hole on the horizon." Faith is typically summoned in the face of darkness, as a means of warding it off, not "pulled" from the darkness, and certainly not from that of a black hole.[40] Still, the stanza ends with a revelatory moment, "I hear your voice calling me," followed immediately by the cry "let it rain!" repeated seven times. It is not clear whether "let it rain" is the content the voice speaks to the singer or the singer's own words, but in either case, it is a cry for a purifying rain after the darkness.

But then the chorus arrives and the tone changes completely: "Meet me at Mary's place, we're gonna have a party!" Both the content and the language are casual and familiar, an allusion to Sam Cooke's "Meet Me at Mary's Place," about a party where "you're gonna have a good time."[41] The singer does not identify Mary, nor, it seems, does he need to; his addressee knows Mary and is familiar with her home. The colloquial "we're gonna have a party" affirms the loose, celebratory feel of the gathering. The black hole in the sun, the sighing angels, the Buddha, the prophet, and the singer's search for faith, have all receded from view. Only the ambiguous question that concludes the chorus hints that more solemn matters are still simmering beneath the surface: "Tell me how do you get this thing started?" The query might be the singer wondering how to get the party started—a perfectly plausible interpretation given the context—but it might also bespeak a concern about moving forward in a deeper, as of yet unarticulated sense.

The next stanza continues the celebratory tone of the chorus, with the singer describing the familiar faces around him, the laughter, "furniture's out on the front porch, music's up loud." But it is not *only* a party when he tells an unidentified addressee"—most likely the same person whose voice called out to him at the end of the first stanza—"your loving grace surrounds me. Irrespective its source, "loving grace"

[40] Strictly speaking, nothing can be pulled from a black hole.

[41] The song appeared on Sam Cooke's *Ain't That Good News* (RCA Victor, 1964).

belongs to a different, more spiritual register than the romantic love and camaraderie of a rowdy get-together, with the furniture pushed out to the porch in order to clear the living room for dancing. But any attempt at a spiritual interpretation is complicated by the words that immediately follow, "I dream of you in my arms," a stock rock 'n' roll phrase of longing for an absent lover. The result is baffling. The singer describes a dance, locates "your loving grace" in its midst, then dreams of holding "you in my arms." Assuming the addressee is the same, the singer is either describing his lover in religiously evocative language ("loving grace"), or describing a female religious figure (Mary?) in physically intimate terms ("you in my arms").

The chorus that follows contains an interesting variation. Instead of "how do you get this thing started?" the singer asks "how do you live broken-hearted?" a question that bridges the party of the second stanza and the spiritual tone of the first—the party at Mary's place is somehow a response to his broken heart. The singer is evidently struggling to get something other than the party started, and if the opening lines of the next stanza are any indication, it is of a religious nature. "I got a picture of you in my locket," the singer states, then describes the locket as a light that guides him through the darkness, while he sets seven candles in his window to light the way for the woman. This is typically Marian imagery: the Virgin Mary is the only female figure regularly featured in lockets, and the seven candles are likely an allusion to the traditional Seven Joys of Mary or, perhaps, to her Seven Sorrows. But just when these lines appear to provide firm evidence that the song addresses the Virgin Mary, the singer, in what seems to be the signature move of this song, pivots from the religious to the secular, and then back. First to the secular: "your favorite record's on the turntable," so clearly he cannot be speaking to the Virgin Mother. Then back to the religious: "I drop the needle and pray" (instead of the expected *play*). The stanza finally returns to the secular, the band "countin' out midnight" and "waitin' for that shout from the crowd."

At first blush, it appears no single interpretation can adequately capture the way "Mary's Place" zigs and zags from the religious realm to the secular, and back again. On the one hand, the song is laden with religious imagery that suggests the title character is the Virgin Mother: the prophet, Buddha, the singer trying to "pull faith" from the black hole in the sun, and the woman's voice calling him; the woman's loving grace, her locket whose light leads him through the dark; and the seven candles in the window to light her way. On the other hand, much of the song actively resists this interpretation. The singer invites us to Mary's place because "we're gonna have a party" filled with familiar faces and laughter; he dreams of holding the woman in his arms—an act of romantic desire, not pious adoration; and he has her favorite record on the turntable. The song not only contains secular and religious images, it interweaves them through sudden shifts from one realm to the other.

The apparent inconsistency is not a shortcoming, but rather the very theme of "Mary's Place," that is, the interpenetration of the sacred and the profane. Rock 'n' roll is a form of religious worship, and religious worship is a form of rock 'n' roll; romantic love is a form of religious adoration, and religious adoration is a form of romantic love; the call and response of the singer and the crowd is a gospel choir, and the quest for spiritual truth can pass through the Buddha and the angels on its way to friendship and music; dropping a record on the turntable is a prayer; the community that forms around music and dance is a church; and recognizing the interrelation of the two is, perhaps, redemption.

Note: Riders on the Train

As we saw above, "Human Touch" affirms the importance of human contact even as the song accepts the modest redemptive force of physical companionship. Love is risky but shutting oneself off from the possibility of love is worse. As the singer says to the woman he is wooing:

> You can't shut off the risk and pain
> Without losin' the love that remains
> We're all riders on this train

The last line in this excerpt repays close examination, as it signals two related shifts in Springsteen's later writings. One involves the referent of the first-person pronoun. Most of Springsteen's songs are written in the first person—the singular referring to the singer, the plural to the singer and his current or potential lover. "Human Touch" contains instances of both (italics are mine throughout): "*I* ain't lookin' for no prayers or pity" alongside "you and me *we* were the pretenders." This pattern appears throughout Springsteen's work.[42] The *we* of "we're all riders on this train," however, does not refer to the singer and the woman he is wooing, but rather invokes humanity as a whole.

This is not the earliest instance of the first-person plural in this sense, since the singer in "Reason to Believe" is speaking for humanity when he asks God to "tell us what does it mean."[43] But after "Human Touch," the collective sense of *we* becomes much more prominent, whether referring to all humankind or to the broader community: "though our bodies lie alone here in the dark, our spirits rise … *we* are alive" ("We Are Alive"), "*we* take care of our own" ("We Take Care of Our Own,"),[44] "*we* sent

---

[42] A few examples include: "*I* think I really dug her … *we* closed our eyes and said goodbye" ("Spirit in the Night"); "*I* wanna guard your dreams and vision … *we* could break this trap" ("Born to Run"); "*I* can't saw that I am sorry for the things that *we* done" ("Nebraska"); "*We* said we'd walk together baby … *I'll* wait for you" ("If I Should Fall Behind"), and many more could be cited.

[43] See the discussion above, chapter four.

[44] Though the song is a critique of America's failure to live up to this motto, the *we* remains collective.

our sons to Korea and Vietnam" ("Youngstown"), and more. This is not to suggest that the romantic *we* disappears, but rather that alongside it there emerges a second *we* that is largely absent from Springsteen's early writings: the community, the nation, or even humanity itself.

The second shift evident in the line involves the train on which we are all riders. George Yamin has rightly noted that in *Born to Run* and other early works "the car (or motorcycle) is for Springsteen a symbol of great religious importance."[45] I argued in chapter three that *Darkness on the Edge of Town* denudes driving of its redemptive powers, representing it as pointless ("chasing some mirage"), violent ("a head on collision"), or desperate ("headin' straight into the storm"). Still, in *The River* and *Nebraska*, the car maintains its symbolic significance, usually as a medium for solitary rumination. Thus we find the singer in "Stolen Car" (*The River*) driving and thinking about the gradual dissolution of his marriage; the driver in "Wreck on the Highway" (*The River*), who comes upon an accident and is forced to recognize the fragility of life; and the drivers in "State Trooper" and "Open All Night" (both *Nebraska*), contemplating their lives as they drive into the night.

Whether a vehicle of redemption or rumination, the car is an individual space. The train, by contrast, is mentioned only rarely in Springsteen's earlier writing, and generally carries negative overtones. For the fish lady in "New York Serenade" (*The Wild, the Innocent & the E Street Shuffle*), the train is more as an obstacle than a mode of transportation: "she won't take the train, she's afraid them tracks are gonna slow her down." In "Downbound Train" (*Born in the U.S.A.*), the singer describes the gradual unraveling of his life as feeling "like a rider on a downbound train"; and the singer in "Leavin' Train" (a *Human Touch* outtake; released on *Tracks*) says "your eyes look like a leavin' train, yeah, they keep on dragging me down."[46] The plaintive "we're all riders on the train" in "Human Touch" introduces a different perspective, as the singer identifies, and asks the woman to identify, as train riders, precisely

---

[45] Yamin, "The Theology of Bruce Springsteen," 10.

[46] Even the upbeat Steel Mill "Train Song," whose singer is eager to reach his destination, ends with a dark twist: "Before you know it I'll be there, and I'll be waltzing arm in arm, with my darling electric chair."

because the train is an aggregate of different people, travels along a fixed route, and has a final destination. Precisely because, in other words, it is a more compelling analogue than the car to the collective and, broadly speaking, predetermined course of human life.[47]

"Human Touch" is not an isolated instance of this more positive attitude toward the train. As I argued above, "Living Proof" suggests that earthly happiness is intimately tied with our ability live in peace with our own finitude. After celebrating the birth of their son in unapologetically religious language ("a little piece of the Lord's undying light"), the singer turns to his wife:

> Tonight let's lie beneath the eaves
> Just a close band of happy thieves
> And when that train comes we'll get on board
> And steal what we can from the treasures, treasures of the Lord

Line three is ambiguous. Is the train also arriving "tonight," or in the more distant future? I cannot say for certain, but it is possible that the line demarcates the limits of this-worldly salvation. Though the child's birth has graced the singer and his wife, "Living Proof" mobilizes the train metaphor to emphasize that theirs is a human, that is, finite joy, and that they recognize and accept that one day they will, metaphorically speaking, have to board the train. Whatever its precise meaning, the valence of the train is positive—it is the vehicle that indicates the family's recognition and acceptance of their mortal limitations, as it carries the family members to the place where they can steal the treasures of the Lord. The association of the train with mortality is explicit in "What Love Can Do" (*Working on a Dream*): "Darling we can't stop this train, when it comes crashing through, but let me show you what love can do." And the communal aspect of the train is highlighted in "Land of Hopes and Dreams" (*Wrecking Ball)*, a conscious counterweight to the train in

---

[47] The shift toward the communal affects the car as well. In "Last to Die" (*Magic*), the car is not the vehicle of an individual, but of a family: "The kids asleep in the backseat, we're just countin' the miles you and me."

"This Train," discussed in chapter one. That train "don't carry nothing but the righteous and the holy," while Springsteen's train "carries saints and sinners ... losers and winners . . . whores and gamblers." Theologically, then, Springsteen offers an inclusive vision of redemption, rejecting the earlier song's notion that freedom from sin is a precondition for ridership on the train. These transitions, first from the car as a vehicle of salvific mobility to a vehicle of contemplation, and then from the car to the train, embody the shift in Springsteen's writing, as a triumphalist celebration of the open road gives way to a muted but still joyful appreciation of the grace available to us in the here-and-now of our lives.

CHAPTER SIX

The Struggle Within

Treating sin and grace in separate chapters might give the impression that Springsteen considers each in isolation, but this is not the case, as a number of songs deal with the internal struggle to hew to what is right and avoid doing what is bad or evil. "Living Proof," discussed in the previous chapter, is at bottom a conversion narrative about such a struggle, recounting the singer's fallen past as a foil to his redeemed present. But the song's narrative begins after the transition is complete—the singer recalls his past from the vantage point of one who has already overcome his difficulties. The present chapter, which examines songs that focus on the struggle to do so, distinguishes between two approaches in Springsteen's work. One frames the struggle as the result of a bifurcation within human nature itself; the other, more common approach, explores fundamentally good individuals confronted with difficult circumstances that may cause them to turn away from their better nature.

"Two Faces" *(Tunnel of Love)*

The idea that human beings are made up of both good and evil forces has its roots in the Hebrew Bible. The first reference to an irredeemably evil aspect of mankind is found just prior to God's decision to bring a flood upon the earth: "The Lord saw that the wickedness of humankind was great in the earth, and that *every* inclination of the thoughts of their hearts was *only* evil continually" (Genesis 6:5). This statement offers a fairly dour view of human beings as creatures whose "every inclination … was only evil continually."[1] Despite this characterization, the notion of an indwelling inclination toward evil does not feature prominently in the Hebrew Bible, and the idea lies dormant until the second and first centuries BCE, when it assumes increasing theological importance. There is no need to examine this idea in all its permutations, except to point to the emergence of a view of the human soul as engaged in a struggle with an evil inclination that pushes the individual toward sin, a struggle sometimes undertaken with the aid of an opposed, positive inclination.[2] Thus the Dead Sea Scrolls, a collection of ancient Hebrew writings dating to the period under discussion, admonish "let not the plan of an evil inclination mislead you"[3] and to "not allow yourselves to be attracted by the thoughts of a guilty inclination and lascivious eyes. For many had gone astray due to these."[4] The second-century CE text *The Shepherd of Hermas* balances the evil inclination with a righteous counterpart, identifying an angel of righteousness and an angel

---

[1] God assesses humanity in very similar terms after the flood ends and Noah and his family have disembarked: "I will never again curse the ground because of humankind, for the inclination of the human heart is evil from youth; nor will I ever again destroy every living creature as I have done" (Genesis 8:21). The reiteration of the motif is curious, in so far as the evil inclination is first invoked to justify the flood, and then to justify God's vow to never again visit such destruction upon humankind.

[2] See Ishay Rosen-Zvi, *Demonic Desires:* Yetzer Hara *and the Problem of Evil in Late Antiquity* (Philadelphia: University of Pennsylvania Press, 2011).

[3] 4Q Instruction (4Q417 2 ii 12), in Florentino García Martínez and Eibert J. C. Tigchelaar, editors, *The Dead Sea Scrolls: Study Edition* (2 vols; Leiden: Brill, 1997), 2.861-862.

[4] Damascus Document (CD-A ii 16-17), in García Martínez and Tigchelaar, *The Dead Sea Scrolls*, 1.552-3; see the discussion of both Dead Sea Scrolls passages in Rosen-Zvi, *Demonic Desires*, 46-50.

of wickedness that reside within man.[5] Most significantly, this is the view championed in several of Paul's letters, the classic example being his harrowing description in the Epistle to the Romans of a man who feels his actions are not his own:

> I do not understand my own actions. For I do not do what I want, but I do the very thing I hate ... in fact it is no longer I that do it, but sin that dwells within me. For I know that nothing good dwells within me, that is, in my flesh. I can will what is right, but I cannot do it. For I do not do the good I want, but the evil I do not want is what I do. Now if I do what I do not want, it is no longer I who do it, but sin that dwells within me. (Romans 7:15-20)

There is vigorous debate among scholars whether Paul intends these statements as a description of his own state, or as a rhetorical "personification" of another speaker.[6] But there is no question that later readers have tended to interpret this passage as an authentic description of Paul's psychological struggle, and that, as a result of Paul's incalculable influence, this view has served as the basis for a Christian view of man as the site of constant internal struggle.[7]

Several songs hint at a state of internal struggle when they contrast the singer's first-person actions or statements with broader claims about the human condition. "Prove It All Night" opens with the singer's optimistic pronouncement, "I've been working real hard trying to get my hands clean," but suggests this effort may be for naught since "everybody's got a hunger they can't resist." The singer in "Hungry Heart" abandons his wife and children ("Got a wife and kids in Baltimore, Jack, I went out for

[5] See the discussion in Rosen-Zvi, *Demonic Desires*, 55-56.

[6] For a summary of the rhetorical position, see John Gager, *Reinventing Paul* (Oxford and New York: Oxford University Press, 2000), 71-73.

[7] See also Greeley's comments in "Catholic Imagination," 237-9. Paul Contino's discussion of the "restless heart" motif in St. Augustin's *Confessions* in his paper "The Theology of St. Augustine and Bruce Springsteen: 'Everybody's Got a Hungry Heart'" demonstrates that similar themes can be found in the works of this important theologian as well. I thank Prof. Contino for sharing his work with me.

a ride and I never went back"), and so finds himself trapped between two incompatible aspects of the human condition. His actions accord with the view that "everybody's got a hungry heart," but are at odds with the last stanza: "Everybody needs a place to rest, everybody wants to have a home." Indeed, when the singer insists that it "don't make no difference what nobody says, ain't nobody wants to be alone," he is imploring the listeners to disregard, first and foremost, the evidence of his own actions.

What is intimated in "Prove It All Night" and "Hungry Heart" is foregrounded in several songs in *Tunnel of Love*. Indeed, "Two Faces" is thoroughly Pauline in its portrayal of a man struggling with his commitment to and love for a woman, so much so that he carries within him two mutually hostile selves.[8] The song opens with a brief description of a love gone bad—the singer swore he would make his girl happy, but he made her cry—and immediately offers a pithy explanation: "two faces have I." The faces in question are not (or: not only) psychological; they cannot be reduced to mood swings or even a persistent sense of self-alienation, but rather two faces correspond to two separate entities.

> One that laughs, one that cries
> One says hello, one says good-bye
> One does things I don't understand
> Makes me feel like half a man

The singer carries within him a foreign entity (or, from the perspective of the other, is himself a foreign entity), another man whose actions he cannot fathom. The statement that the other "face" does things that "I

[8] Despite some thematic similarities, "Brilliant Disguise," another song from *Tunnel of Love*, does not make the same claim. There the singer tries and ultimately fails to distinguish the real self from the merely apparent both in his lover and in himself: "So when you look at me, you better look hard and look twice, is that me baby, or just a brilliant disguise?" Though the picture of the divided self is superficially similar, in "Brilliant Disguise" it is the result of the dynamics of the relationship at a given time rather than to a struggle between two internal forces. The same is true of the inspiration for "Two Faces," Lou Christie's 1963 hit "Two Faces Have I," whose singer pretends to be happy so that the world will not see his heartache. This is a deliberate act ("I pretend that I'm happy, but I'm Mr. Blue; I pretend that I'm happy, since I lost you"), not a schism within the singer's being.

don't understand," echoes Paul's "I do not understand my own actions. For I do not do what I want, but I do the very thing I hate" (Romans 7:15). Such a deep bifurcation makes it impossible to construe the first-person pronoun "I" as a straightforward reference to the speaker. Paul recognizes this by identifying the aspect of himself that does God's will as an "inner man" that clashes with his own body: "For I delight in the law of God in my inner man, but I see in my members another law at war with the law of my mind, making me captive to the law of sin that dwells in my members" (Romans 7:22-23). In similar fashion, the singer in "Two Faces" despairs of his internal war, complaining, in an elegant turn of phrase, of feeling "like half a man." Typically a cliché of male inadequacy, the phrase is in this case literally true, since the singer—the "face" or self that sings "Two Faces"—coexists in a single body with another self, and so constitutes only half a man.

The focus of the struggle between the two faces is the woman to whom the song is addressed. However, the struggle is not driven by the dynamics of the relationship. The woman has not done anything to incite the antagonism of the other face, nor is there any suggestion that she could somehow help placate it. How could she? The issue is not her behavior but rather the division that splits the man into two entities. It's not you; it's us. As a consequence, there is no hope for a permanent resolution. The singer can pray that "our love will make that other man go away," and the song ends with an optimistic willingness to fight the other man for the relationship ("well, go ahead and let him try"); but there is also a somber recognition that the struggle is permanent: "he'll never say goodbye."

"Cautious Man" *(Tunnel of Love)*

The titular cautious man is Billy Horton, whose caution first wavers then collapses when he meets, loves, and marries a young woman. But the love Billy feels does not overcome the duality of his nature, visually represented by the tattoos "love" on his right hand and "fear" on his left. Fearing the restlessness in his own heart, Billy prays for steadiness but one night, he awakens from a terrible nightmare and, though his wife lies asleep by his side, he feels as though she is irretrievably distant. He gets out of bed, dresses, and walks down to the highway. The situation is grim but not hopeless. Billy's love for his wife is true and he wants to do what is right, but he also knows that, as Paul wrote, sometimes "I do not do the good I want, but the evil I do not want is what I do" (Romans 7:19). Billy cannot quell his heart's restlessness, he is not powerless against it, and in another critique of the road theology, realizes that the highway offers escape, not redemption, for "when he got there he didn't find nothing but road."[9]

Perhaps Billy realizes, fully and finally, that salvation does not await him elsewhere, or perhaps he merely wins a temporary victory and is doomed to forever struggle with his inner fears. Whatever the case, Billy returns home and the song ends with a moment of grace: "At their bedside he brushed the hair from his wife's face as the moon shone on her skin so white, filling their room with the beauty of God's fallen light." Billy has battled his internal demons and, at least for now, remained true to his wife and to himself. His prayers for steadiness have been answered, and as he returns to his wife's side, the room is bathed in God's light. But the concluding line is not altogether redemptive, as much hangs on the word *fallen*. It could mean that the light has fallen down from the heavens into Billy's bedroom, amplifying the revelatory force of the moment. But *fallen* can also refer to mankind's state following original sin, in which case the divine light is fallen in so far as it reflects the fallenness of human existence, the fundamental rupture within us into love, on the one hand, and hate, on the other.

"Galveston Bay" *(The Ghost of Tom Joad)*

"Two Faces" and "Cautious Man" represent the struggle within as the result of man's riven nature. This view, however, does not recur outside of *Tunnel of Love*. Springsteen more often represents the struggle as that of individuals faced with difficult external circumstances that force them

[9] Greeley makes a similar point in "Catholic Imagination," 238.

to either affirm their better selves or succumb to hatred or fear. In this, Springsteen naturalizes sin and grace, making them part (or a potential part) of the very fabric of our lives.

"Galveston Bay" tells the story of two fishermen in a Texas town. Le Bin Son is a Vietnamese man who fought alongside United States forces in the war and brought his family to America after the fall of Saigon, and Billy Sutter is a wounded Vietnam War veteran whose xenophobia grows fiercer as Vietnamese refugees settle in the region. Three unnamed men try to burn down the Vietnamese fishing boats, and Le kills two of them. Though the court acquits Le on grounds of self-defense, Billy vows revenge and one night, he goes down to the waterside, knife in hand, to kill Le:

> Le lit a cigarette, the bay was still as glass
> As he walked by, Billy stuck his knife in his pocket
> Took a breath and let him pass

"Galveston Bay" does not explore the tempest raging within Billy's soul, but it is clear that he is at an existential crossroads—succumb to hatred and kill Le or return home to his family? He chooses the latter, and is rewarded with a moment of quotidian grace: "Billy ... kissed his sleeping wife ... And cast his nets into the water of Galveston Bay."[10] This last image, and the language of "casting nets" in particular, echoes the New Testament description of Jesus' first disciples: "As he walked by the Sea of Galilee, he saw two brothers, Simon, who is called Peter, and Andrew his brother, casting a net into the sea—for they were fishermen" (Matthew 4:18). Overcoming the murderous urge in his heart and pulling away from violence, Billy Sutter too follows Christ.

[10] In a later interview, Springsteen described Billy Sutter's decision as a type of miracle: "Then I had this idea of writing a song ... about a guy who makes a particular decision not to add to the brutality and violence ... That's a miracle that can happen, that does happen. People get to a certain brink, and they make a good choice, instead of a deadly choice." David Corn, "Bruce Springsteen Tells the Story of the Secret America," *Mother Jones* (March/April, 1996); reprinted in Burger, *Springsteen on Springsteen*, 216. Note how Springsteen transforms the concept of a miracle, traditionally defined as an event contrary to the natural order, into a natural occurrence.

"Streets of Philadelphia" *(Philadelphia Soundtrack)*

"Streets of Philadelphia," written for Jonathan Demme's 1993 film about the social and professional ostracism suffered by an AIDS patient, is a first-person account of an ill man seeking acceptance. An unnamed disease is consuming the singer, who speaks of being bruised and battered, unable to recognize his own reflection. Contemplating his physical decline, the singer makes two interconnected theological assertions: "ain't no angel gonna greet me, it's just you and I my friend"—the world is bereft of divine grace, but some form of interpersonal redemption may be possible.

Much of the song is devoted to the singer's uncertainty whether the community or man he addresses will accept him. The singer walks through the streets of the city hearing "the voices of friends vanished and gone," many doubtless having succumbed to the same disease, but some perhaps vanished because they turned their back on him. He cries out: "Oh brother are you gonna leave me wastin' away, on the streets of Philadelphia?" The inclusion of the city's name is intentional (as it is in the movie), since *philadelphia* is Greek for "brotherly love," and the city was founded by William Penn as a civic manifestation of this ideal.[11] How terrible if the singer were abandoned to die by his brothers, in the city of brotherly love.

"Streets of Philadelphia" is dotted with religious references. Addressing his fellow man as *brother* is typical for male cohorts of a religious community. As Jesus says when told that his mother and brothers wish to speak with him: "'Who is my mother, and who are my brothers?' And pointing to his disciples, he said, 'Here are my mother and my brothers! For whoever does the will of my Father in heaven is my brother and sister and mother'" (Matthew 12:46-50).[12] Of course, the singer has already stated that no angel will greet him, and he does not

[11] "As a Quaker, Penn envisioned a place of refuge for the persecuted, where the spiritual union of all Christians might be more than a dream. He intended to live at peace with the Indians, so he made no provision for city walls or fortifications or garrisons of soldiers ... In short, Penn wanted his city of brotherly love to be radically different from any other town in the Western world." Mary Maples Dunn and Richard S. Dunn, "The Founding: 1681-1701," in Russel F. Weigley, editor, *Philadelphia: A 300-Year History* (New York and London: Norton, 1982), 1-2.

[12] The religious title *friar* is a late form of the Latin *frater*, "brother."

hope for the salvation of his soul or ascent to heaven. Yet he does hold out hope for the redemptive power of acceptance by his fellow man, by his brother. As he feels himself dying, he pleads:

> So receive me brother with your faithless kiss,
> Or will we leave each other alone like this
> On the Streets of Philadelphia

These lines are suffused with religious imagery. The phrase "receive me brother" alludes to receiving communion, or the Eucharist, a church sacrament based on the account of Christ's disciples eating the bread he calls his flesh, and drinking the wine he calls his blood.[13] Each individual member of the congregation ritually consumes the bread and wine, but the experience is communal. Indeed, according to John Paul II's encyclical (papal letter) on the Eucharist, it is fraternal:

> The gift of Christ and his Spirit which we receive in Eucharistic communion superabundantly fulfils the yearning for fraternal unity deeply rooted in the human heart; at the same time it elevates the experience of fraternity already present in our common sharing at the same Eucharistic table to a degree which far surpasses that of the simple human experience of sharing a meal.[14]

Fraternity is precisely what the singer requests in addressing his brother. Phrased differently, the singer is asking to remain part of the (non-ecclesiastical) congregation; he is asking not to be excommunicated, that is, denied membership in his community through the withholding of communion.[15]

---

[13] See the discussion of "Lost in the Flood" in chapter one, above.

[14] John Paul II, *Ecclesia de Eucharistia*[Encyclical letter on the Eucharist in its Relation to the Church], section 24; accessed August 18, 2015: http://w2.vatican.va/content/john-paul-ii/en/encyclicals/documents/hf_jp-ii_enc_20030417_eccl-de-euch.html.

[15] See Springsteen's comments in his interview to Judy Wieder in *The Advocate* (April 2, 1996); reprinted in Phillips and Masur, *Talk About a Dream*, 209: "Q: When there are walls between people and there is a lack of acceptance, you can reach for that particular kind of communion: 'Receive me, brother' is the lyric in the last verse. A: That's all anybody's asking for."

Communion, moreover, is an act of great physical intimacy, as the consumption of bread and wine by the faithful is tantamount to accepting Christ into their body. The theological doctrines that underlie this act have been contested for centuries, with Protestant churches holding that bread and wine do not become a different substance, but rather are accompanied by Christ's presence (a doctrine known as consubstantiation), while Catholics (along with the Eastern Orthodox Church and others) counter that the consumed wine and wafer are transformed, in actual reality, into the blood and flesh of Christ (transubstantiation). Particularly on the Catholic understanding, to receive communion is, in a very literal sense, to assimilate the flesh and blood of Christ into one's body. As John Paul II writes: "The saving efficacy of the sacrifice is fully realized when the Lord's body and blood are received in communion ... we receive his body which he gave up for us on the Cross and his blood which he 'poured out for many for the forgiveness of sins' (Matthew 26:28)."[16] The singer in "Streets of Philadelphia" asks that he too be accepted with similar intimacy. "Receive me," that is, receive my body—though it is the body of a gay man; receive my blood—though it carries the disease.[17]

The singer's request to be received with a kiss has a twofold effect. First, the song's context precludes a sexual interpretation of the act, and so Springsteen endows the singer with a core humanity that cannot be reduced to the overwrought cliché of a hypersexual gay man.[18] Second, the request invokes the kisses with which early followers of Jesus greeted one another. In the conclusion to his First Letter to the Corinthians, Paul asks that the members of the congregation "greet one another with a holy kiss" (1 Corinthians 14-20), and he repeats the request at the end of his second letter to the same congregation (2 Corinthians 13:11-12).[19] In

---

[16] John Paul II, *Ecclesia de Eucharistia*, sec. 16.

[17] Springsteen notes: "If my work was about anything, it was about the search for identity, for personal recognition, for acceptance, for *communion*, and for a big country," Judy Wieder interview in *The Advocate*; reprinted in Phillips and Masur, *Talk About a Dream*, 211; emphasis added.

[18] The singer's plea for kiss from his brother echoes an earlier request from "This Hard Land" (a *Born in the U.S.A.* outtake released on *Tracks*), where the male singer promises: "Just one kiss from you my brother and we'll ride until we fall."

[19] Se also 1 Thessalonians 5:26. The infamous kiss by which Judas identified Jesus to the Roman authorities (see Matthew 26:48-49) does not fit the context of "Streets of Philadelphia."

similar fashion, the singer appeals for a kiss that will mark him as a member of a congregation. But even in the face of imminent death, the singer does not ground his request in a religious or transcendent justification, asking to be received with a *faithless* kiss. This is a congregation founded on the grace of man, not of God.

"Streets of Philadelphia" is primarily concerned with the singer's yearning for acceptance. He knows that he is dying ("I can feel myself fading away") and wants desperately to remain part of his secular congregation, his brotherhood. The internal struggle takes place within the man whom the song addresses, who is faced with a momentous choice: to accept the dying man in an act of grace, or abandon him. Not one but two lives hang in the balance: "will we leave *each other* alone like this?" If the brother turns his back on the dying singer, he will be betraying himself as well; he too will be left alone, on the streets of Philadelphia.

"Spare Parts" *(Tunnel of Love)*

If "Streets of Philadelphia" ends without resolution, "Spare Parts" reaches its poetic apex at the moment of decision. Janey becomes pregnant by her boyfriend, Bobby, who promises to marry her but instead walks out. Left to care for her newborn son, Janey sinks into depression, and in this vulnerable state hears about a woman who drowned her baby in the river. Janey takes her own son to the river, presumably intending to kill him, but "waist deep in the water, how bright the sun shone, she lifted him in her arms and carried him home."[20]

The song opens with a trenchant theological claim: "Bobby said he'd pull out, Bobby stayed in, Janey had a baby, it wasn't any sin," a statement that is at once a rejection of the traditional Catholic condemnation of premarital sex, and an affirmation of the understanding of sin as a surrender to negative circumstances, since Janey's pregnancy is nothing of the sort. To the contrary, it is the result of trusting her lover's promises of responsible sexual behavior and, later, of his commitment to her and to

[20] The reference to the sun's brightness may play on the homonyms "sun" and "son," a reading suggested to me by Neil Patton.

their child. Janey erred in trusting Bobby, but she did not sin. What she contemplates in the river, however, *is* a sin, both in the traditional sense and in the particular meaning Springsteen gives the term, as allowing external difficulties to overcome hope.

Commenting on Janey's entry into the river, Andrew Greeley asserts it "is surely a baptismal image. How could it be anything else?"[21] But Greeley misses a key point. Baptism is a meticulously scripted ritual that takes place at an appointed time and consists of fixed actions and pronouncements. The poetic power of "Spare Parts" lies precisely in not knowing how things will turn out. Janey, betrayed and abandoned, crippled by post-partum depression, may allow her baby to sink to its death (and perhaps follow him into the river's depths), or she may carry her child out of the river to resume their life together. Since she chooses the latter, the immersion in the river does become baptismal—in that Greeley is right—but his rhetorical question "how could it be anything else?" is misguided. The symbolic power of the river lies in its being only potentially baptismal, and potentially the site of infanticide and suicide. Moreover, to characterize Janey's action as a baptism diverts our focus from the character being saved. The sacrament of baptism is concerned with the salvation of the infant, and though there is an infant in the river, it is the adult, Janey, not the child, who emerges transformed. Transformed, it should further be noted, by her inner fortitude and determination, not by divine grace.

Janey's redemption, moreover, is thoroughly this-worldly. While her baby sleeps back home, Janey takes her wedding dress and engagement ring and "went straight down to the pawnshop, man, and walked out with some good cold cash." Janey's action is unflinchingly anti-romantic. The ring and the dress are the quintessential reminders of her relationship with Bobby. Under normal circumstances, pawning them would count as a dramatic devaluation—their cherished symbolic worth exchanged for debased cash. But "Spare Parts," which may contain rock 'n' roll's most unromantic account of conception ("Bobby said he'd pull out, Bobby

[21] Greeley, "Catholic Imagination," 239. Matthew Orel claims that the Binding of Isaac is the relevant biblical intertext, but while "Spare Parts" shares the theme of filicide, I do not think Orel's view finds support in the language of the song. See Orel, "From Adam to Jesus," 150.

stayed in"), is steadfast in its refusal of romanticism. Janey grasps the true exchange rate: the ring and the dress were never worth more than the pawnbroker price since, absent true commitment from Bobby, they were worthless from the outset. Janey exits the pawnshop with cash—*cold* cash, the song emphasizes—and so demonstrates that she has recognized her new reality, made her peace with it, and begun to build a better future for herself and her child.

"Paradise" *(The Rising)*

A lyrically complex song, "Paradise," like "Spare Parts," culminates in a woman contemplating drowning herself in a river.[22] The song consists of three scenes, each two stanzas long, narrated in the first-person, though not by the same character.[23] The first describes a suicide bomber removing the books from his child's backpack, filling it with explosives, kissing the child ("the breath of eternity on your lips"), and then proceeding to a crowded marketplace, where he looks at the faces of his victims and "wait[s] for paradise"—a martyr's death. The second scene introduces a new speaker who remarks on the beauty of the Virginia hills and describes visiting their beloved in a dream, the feel of their hair, their smell, and the touch of their skin: "I taste the void upon your lips, and I wait for paradise." The final stanza recounts a scene that is very similar to the conclusion of "Spare Parts." The speaker searches for a beloved "on the other side, where the river runs clean and wide," and then enters the waters.

> I sink 'neath the river cool and clear
> Drifting down I disappear
> I see you on the other side
> I search for the peace in your eyes
> But they're as empty as paradise

[22] For a sensitive analysis of "Paradise" and, in particular, the song's relationship to Flannery O'Connor's "The River," see Graybill, "'As Empty as Paradise'," 28-33.
[23] Springsteen used this technique as early as 1970 in "Where Was Jesus in Ohio?" which alternates between the perspective of the demonstrator shot at Kent State ("as my life ends ... And the sun disappears into the night") and that of a National Guardsman ("and the gun they gave me is heavy, hun, and the helmet hurts my head").

In *Songs*, a book of Springsteen's lyrics accompanied by his commentary, Springsteen writes that the first verse depicts "a young Palestinian suicide bomber [who] contemplates his last moments on earth. In the second, a Navy wife longs for her husband lost at the Pentagon … In the last verse, my character swims deep into the waters between worlds where they confront their lost love."[24] Despite the authority of Springsteen's interpretation, I find compelling reasons to read the second and third scenes as depicting different characters—the husband killed in the suicide-bombing and his wife, respectively. One important consideration is the shift that occurs between the fourth stanza (that concludes the second scene) and the beginning of the fifth stanza (that opens the third). After describing the dream visit, the fourth stanza ends with the words "and I wait for paradise, and I wait for paradise," while the fifth opens with "I search for you on the other side." To my mind, these statements bespeak different perspectives, the former resigned and passive, the latter probing and active, suggesting that these are two characters, the husband and wife, respectively. Another consideration is the phrase "I visit you in another dream" in the third stanza. If the wife is dreaming of her dead husband, "I dream of you" (or something along those lines) would be the expected language, but it is common to speak of the dead "visiting" the living in a dream.[25] Note, moreover, the contrast between the "I visit you in another dream" and "I look for you on the other side." The speaker of the former knows precisely where to find the person he seeks but the speaker of the latter is still searching for them, another indication that these are different voices, different characters. While none of these claims is decisive on its own, in aggregate they suggest that the speaker in the second scene (stanzas three and four) is not, *pace* Springsteen, the bereaved wife, but the dead husband, roaming the hills of Virginia, visiting his wife in her dreams, yearning for now impossible physical contact, and hoping for release from this intermediate state—awaiting paradise. On this interpretation, the song is elegantly structured as a series of circles

---

[24] Springsteen, *Songs*, 306. Other interpreters have followed his lead, e.g., Symynkywicz, *The Gospel According to Bruce Springsteen*, 146-7.

[25] The technical name for dreams about deceased loved ones is "visitation dreams."

expanding from the point of attack, depicting first the suicide bomber, then his victim, and finally the victim's wife.

The key moment of the song occurs at its conclusion, which on either interpretation involves the victim's wife. Like Janey in "Spare Parts," the grieving widow enters the river and is tempted to give herself over to its flow. As she drifts down, she has a vision of her husband "on the other side." She probes his eyes to see if they are filled with peace, but find that "they're as empty as paradise." This remarkable simile describes the vacuity both of the husband's eyes and of paradise, effectively countering the suicide bomber's view of paradise as a site of eternal life. For the living, the widow says, paradise is not an alluring reward; it is empty in comparison to the fullness of the world. She also realizes that the temptation of death itself is empty. She will not find peace there, nor will she be reunited with her husband. Although she sees him on the other side, she knows they must go their separate ways, he to the realm of the dead, she to the realm of the living. At that point, she surfaces and the song ends in a beautiful affirmation of the woman's decision:

> I break above the waves
> I feel the sun upon my face

Though her grief is great, frighteningly close to unbearable, the woman ultimately chooses life over death. As she surfaces from the river that moments earlier could have been a cold grave, she feels the warmth of the summer sun on her face—the same sun that shone brightly for Janey in "Spare Parts"—the sheer physical pleasure of the world welcoming her back to the land of the living.

* * *

In concluding this section, I want to return to a poetic principle that informs much of Springsteen's writing. In my discussion of "Spare Parts," I argued against Andrew Greeley's assertion that the river must be a baptismal symbol ("how could it be anything else?"). Greeley's identification is correct, since the river ends up symbolizing a baptism-like rebirth (for Janey, not her infant child), but the river only becomes baptismal when Janey makes her choice. In more technical terms, the river in "Spare Parts" is not a rigid poetic signifier. Its waters could symbolize either rebirth or death, and the dramatic force of the song hinges on the possibility of these different outcomes.

"Spare Parts" is not unique in this regard. A single poetic signifier can produce different, even contradictory meanings, throughout Springsteen's writing. I am not referring to symbolic transformation that reflects a shift in the narrated events, as when, in "The River," the young lovers' river runs dry, mirroring their lost love. Rather, I have in mind the symbolic flexibility exhibited, say, by the concept of the Promised Land, that stands as a salvific destination in "Thunder Road" and "The Promised Land," but denotes an unfulfilled journey, an epic effort that ends in dashed hopes, in "The Price You Pay." Or the way rain symbolizes despair in "Leap of Faith," ("All over the world the rain was pourin' … Oh heartbreak and despair got nothing but boring"), but hope in "Living Proof" ("It's been a long long drought baby, tonight the rain's pourin' down on our roof; looking for a little bit of God's mercy, I found living proof").

The willow is closely linked to the loss of love in both "Brilliant Disguise" ("I heard somebody call your name from underneath our willow") and "Reason to Believe" ("the sun sets behind a weepin' willow tree, groom stands alone and watches the river rush on so effortlessly").[26] But in "Two Faces," the willow appears in a more positive context: "Last night as I kissed you 'neath the willow tree, he swore he'd take your love away from me … Well go ahead and let him try." The narrative appears headed toward another account of lost love, but the willow symbolism of "Brilliant Disguise" and "Reason to Believe" does not determine its meaning here. Although the danger of loss hovers over the encounter, the singer ends with an affirmation of his commitment to his lover. So too the Cadillac in "Pink Cadillac" is a raunchy sexual image, but in

[26] This negative association is likely tied to the willow's propensity for "weeping."

"Adam Raised a Cain," the son's acceptance of his "daddy's Cadillac" is a surrender to a life from which he had hoped to extricate himself.27 And if one were to ask what naming means in Springsteen's work, the only proper response would be: it depends. "Does This Bus Stop at 82nd Street?" identifies naming with blessing: "Hey, bus driver, keep the change, bless your children, give them names." But in "Gave It a Name" (an outtake from *Human Touch* released on *Tracks*), the act is much darker:

In the fields of the lord, stood Abel and Cain
Cain slew Abel 'neath the black rain
At night he couldn't stand the guilt or the blame
So he gave it a name

I argued in chapter three that *Darkness on the Edge of Town* preserves much of *Born to Run*'s poetic lexicon, but transforms and even reverses its meaning, but that some interpreters have failed to recognize the shift, assigning symbolic uniformity to Springsteen's albums.[28] I can now extend the argument and claim that the shift in symbolism from *Born to Run* to *Darkness on the Edge of Town* is typical of a poetic that eschews rigid symbolic meanings, allowing the significance of each symbol to be determined by the mood of the song and its characters' actions.

I have presented this aspect of Springsteen's poetic in some detail because it corresponds, on a literary level, to the internal struggles

---

[27] I discuss "Adam Raised a Cain" in the following section.

[28] It is likely the influence of *Born to Run* that causes interpreters such as Symynkywicz to interpret Springsteen's entire corpus as an unnuanced, life-affirming drive toward redemption. For example, Symynkywicz interprets "Something in the Night"—a song antithetical to the car ethos of *Born to Run*, that describes the driver tearing "into the guts of something in the night" and ending up "running burned and blind"—as an uplifting lesson that we should not "turn our backs on life and give up on our chase for that elusive, inspiring, life-sustaining 'something in the night'" (Symynkywicz, *The Gospel According to Bruce Springsteen*, 50); in "Racing in the Street," the final drive to the sea to "wash these sins off our hands" becomes, in Symynkywicz's interpretation, a drive to "the sea—the great ocean of new possibilities—in whose life-giving waters the sins of the past are washed away and where new hopes for the future are born" (Symynkywicz, *The Gospel According to Bruce Springsteen*, 53); even the desire to "spit in the face of these badlands" is read through rose-tinted glasses: "When we live our lives honestly and faithfully, we 'spit in the face' of those who deride our human race as hopelessly bound to sin and depravity" (Symynkywicz, *The Gospel According to Bruce Springsteen*, 46).

outlined in this chapter, struggles that determine whether a character will fall into sin or be touched by grace: Billy Sutter grappling with his desire to kill Le Bin Son; Billy Horton forever wrestling with the love and fear within him; Janey in “Spare Parts” and the widow in “Paradise” entering a river perhaps never to leave it. The notion that sin is a falling away from our better selves entails that the individual could have acted otherwise, and so we can assume similar struggles take place in other characters. The New Timer agonizing over his friend’s murder; the soldier in “Devils & Dust” proclaiming the justice of his cause in the face of mounting evidence to the contrary; the singer in “My Father’s House” allowing himself to grow further apart from his father in the years preceding the song. With very few exceptions, the fate of Springsteen’s characters is not predetermined. Though external circumstances may press them in a certain direction, they maintain freedom of choice and with it the possibility of either falling into sin or being elevated by grace. In this, the content of Springsteen’s songs accords with his poetic. Just as the characters choose their course of action and thereby determine their fate, the tropes and images in Springsteen’s songs are not predetermined, their symbolic meaning also decided by the actions of the songs’ characters.

Note: Springsteen's Biblical Poetic

The story of the Binding of Isaac, recounted in the twenty-second chapter of Genesis, begins as follows:

> After these things God tested Abraham. He said to him, "Abraham!" And he said, "Here I am." He said, "Take your son, your only son Isaac, whom you love, and go to the land of Moriah, and offer him there as a burnt-offering on one of the mountains that I shall show you." So Abraham rose early in the morning, saddled his donkey, and took two of his young men with him, and his son Isaac; he cut the wood for the burnt-offering, and set out and went to the place in the distance that God had shown him. (Genesis 22:1-3)

The language is sparse and the scene perfunctorily set: the Bible does not contextualize the encounter, nor identify the nature of "these things" after which the test occurs. More importantly, the Bible does not provide a vista into the internal world of the narrative's two main characters—one human, the other divine. Why does God decide to test Abraham, after promising that "I will make of you [Abraham] a great nation, and I will bless you, and make your name great" (Genesis 12:2)? If Abraham fails the test, will God renege on the earlier promise? And, most disturbingly, why does God test Abraham's fidelity by commanding him to slit his son's throat and burn his body? The Bible's silence is still more striking with regard to Abraham. What goes through his mind, and his heart, when he hears God's command? Does he struggle to understand it? Does he doubt God's justice? Does he consider sharing the information with his wife, Sarah, Isaac's mother? The book of Genesis remains silent on all these questions.

This silence, altogether typical of the narrative of the Hebrew Bible, led Erich Auerbach to formulate his famous distinction between the literary styles of Homer and the Bible, according to which Homer provides richly detailed narratives that "represent phenomena in a fully externalized form, visible and palpable,"[29] while in biblical scenes "time and place are undefined and call for interpretation; thoughts and feelings remain unexpressed" with the result that the narrative as a whole is "fraught with background."[30] Phrased differently, much of what Homer places in the foreground, the Bible sets as background—the visual context of a scene, and the thoughts, memories, and feelings of its characters. What Genesis 22 does foreground is, oddly, geography: Abraham is to go to the land of Moriah, a three-day journey, to one of the mountains that God will indicate. The land of Moriah has not been mentioned in the book of Genesis thus far, nor does it appear elsewhere in the Pentateuch. In fact, there is only one other mention of Moriah in the entire Hebrew Bible, in a verse that strains to explain Genesis 22.[31] The result is a curious imbalance. On the one hand, the narrative says little about Abraham's emotional response, even and especially in the face of such harrowing choices; on the other, it provides geographic specificity whose literary function is not clear.

I have introduced Auerbach's thesis because it may illuminate, or at least help to frame, the lyrical shift that occurs in Springsteen's writing in *Darkness on the Edge of Town*. Prior to this album, Springsteen's songs often lead the listener into a densely populated, hyper-specific world of characters and places. Crazy Janey and the mission man on the trip to Greasy Lake ("Spirit in the Night"), Sandy and the boardwalk characters ("4th of July, Asbury Park (Sandy))," Cat, Kitty and Jack Knife ("Kitty's Back"), Spanish Johnny and Puerto Rican Jane ("Incident on 57th Street")—almost all of the songs in *Greetings from Asbury Park, N.J.* and *The Wild, the Innocent & the E Street Shuffle* adopt this narrative style.

[29] Erich Auerbach, "Odysseus's Scar," in his *Mimesis: The Representation of Reality in Western Literature*, translated by Willard Trask (New York: Doubleday, 1953), 6.
[30] Auerbach, *Mimesis*, 11-12.
[31] According to the author of Chronicles, "Solomon began to build the house of the Lord in Jerusalem on Mount Moriah" (2 Chronicles 3:1). This is a late tradition that tries to make sense of the land of Moriah in the Abraham narrative by recasting it as Mount Moriah, now identified as the mountain on which the Jerusalem Temple is constructed. Note that in Genesis, God tells Abraham to go to the land of Moriah, to a mountain that will be specified, so Moriah is not originally the name of the mountain but of the region that houses the unnamed mountain.

Born to Run is less uniform, as "Night" and "She's the One" never identify their locations and protagonists, but many of the album's songs maintain the earlier style: Terry and the singer on the beach at Stockton Wing ("Backstreets"), the adventures of Bad Scooter and Big Man in "Tenth Avenue Freeze-Out,"[32] the Rat and the barefoot girl in "Jungleland,"—all concrete characters in specific settings.

Beginning with *Darkness on the Edge of Town*, Springsteen adopts a style that resonates with the Hebrew Bible's combination of minimal emotional description and geographic specificity. Springsteen often introduces distressing events (lost love, more often than not) with complete detachment. In the opening lines of "Hungry Heart" (*The River*)—"Got a wife and kids in Baltimore, Jack, I went out for a ride and I never went back"—the singer casually mentions his family, and informs us that he abandoned them all, never to return. The almost off-hand reference raises many questions, involving both the external events (What led to this decision? Does the singer maintain contact with his wife and children?) and the ensuing emotional turmoil (How has he dealt with the abandonment? How have they?). But "Hungry Heart" is uninterested in such matters. Other songs, too, communicate great loss with extreme brevity: "I had a job, I had a girl, I had something going, mister, in this world; I got laid off down at the lumber yard, our love went bad, time's got hard";[33] "I met a girl and we ran away, I swore I'd make her happy every day, and how I made her cry";[34] "Times were tough, love was not enough, so you said, 'Sorry Johnny I'm gone gone gone'";[35] and "I lost my money and I lost my wife."[36] These lines are, in Auerbach's wonderful phrase, fraught with background. They allude to dramatic events, to struggles and disappointments and heartbreak, but relegate them all to the unnarrated background.

Yet these same songs often contain surprising geographic details. "Something in the Night" opens with a local reference: "I'm riding down

---

[32] The pseudonym "Bad Scooter" is based, I suspect, on its initials.

[33] "Downbound Train," *Born in the U.S.A.*

[34] "Two Faces," *Tunnel of Love.*

[35] "When You're Alone," *Tunnel of Love.*

[36] "Darkness on the Edge of Town," *Darkness on the Edge of Town.*

Kingsley, figuring I'll get a drink." This line could constitute an intimate invitation into the singer's world, but the song does not develop in this direction, adopting a universal tone, instead: "You're born with nothing, and better off that way, soon as you've got something they send someone to try and take it away." "Darkness on the Edge of Town" (*Darkness on the Edge of Town*) mentions the woman living "up in Fairview" and "spot out 'neath Abrams Bridge." "Stolen Car" (*The River*) describes the collapse of a marriage without mentioning the wife's name or the issues driving the couple apart, but notes that the singer is driving a stolen care "down on Eldridge Avenue." As noted above, "Hungry Heart" is silent about the singer's emotional turmoil, but the song does specify that he abandoned his wife and children in Baltimore, and then meets a woman in Kingstown. Even "The River" (*The River*), set in an almost mythical landscape of "the valley" and "the river" and "the reservoir," is punctuated by the concrete specificity of the singer working "for the Johnstown Company."

Springsteen's later narrative style serves a number of poetic functions. In one sense, it counters Tolstoy's famous statement that all happy families are alike, but every unhappy family is unhappy in its own way. By describing separation and heartbreak in such bare language, Springsteen suggests that unhappiness is also generic. Each failing relationship consists of its own specific circumstances, but ultimately it all boils down to "our love went bad." Also, the psychologically muted lyrics of these songs reflect the internal state of their narrators. The silence of songs like "Racing in the Street," "Hungry Heart," and "Stolen Car" concerning the emotional price of the events they describe, reflects their singers' very limited capacity to recognize and deal with such matters. Finally, it should be noted that the shift in Springsteen's narrative is usually framed in terms of his encounter with country music and the writing of Flannery O'Connor prior to *Darkness on the Edge of Town*. Without diminishing the importance of these aspects, it remains striking that as Springsteen examines questions of sin and salvation, he does so in a poetic form that resonates so clearly with the voice of the Hebrew Bible.

Springsteen's Midrash

CHAPTER SEVEN

Springsteen's Midrash

I did read the Bible some[1]

After Adam and Eve are expelled from the Garden of Eden, the book of Genesis records the following exchange between their two sons: "Cain said to his brother Abel, and when they were in the field, Cain set upon his brother Abel and killed him" (Genesis 4:8).[2] This account contains a perplexing gap, as it omits Cain's words to his brother. The early Greek translation of Genesis, that serves as the basis for most English-language Bibles, offers one possibility: "Cain said to his brother Abel 'Let us go out to the field.' And when they were in the field …" Third and fourth century rabbinic interpreters of the Bible, however, working from the Hebrew version, had to confront the omission, as we find in this commentary to Genesis:

[1] Duncan, "Lawdamercy," 86, discussing the writing of "Adam Raised a Cain"; reprinted in Burger, *Sprinsteen on Springsteen*, 86.
[2] The translation follows the *New Jewish Publication Society* version.

> "Cain said to his brother Abel" (Genesis 4:8): Concerning what did they dispute? They said: come, let us divide the world; one took possession of the lands, the other of the movable objects. The one said, you are standing on my land, and the other said, what you are wearing is mine … and so "Cain rose up against his brother Abel and killed him" (Genesis 4:8). Rabbi Joshua of Sikhnin said … the one said, the temple will be built in my territory, the other said in mine. "And when they were in the field" (Genesis 4:8), the word "field" refers to nothing other than the temple, as it is written "Zion shall be ploughed like a field" (Micah 3:12). And so "Cain rose up against his brother Abel and killed him" (Genesis 4:8) ... [Rabbi] Huna said, a twin girl was born with Abel, and the one said, I will take her, since I am the elder, and the other said, I will take her since she was born with me.[3]

These interpretations are all motivated by the same textual difficulty, each offering an account of Cain's missing words to his brother. At the same time, the rabbinic interpreters are also striving to make sense of the horror of the broader biblical narrative, to explain what might have driven Cain to slay his brother. The latter desire is curious, since the book of Genesis already offers an explanation: after the two brothers make offerings to God, "the Lord had regard for Abel and his offering, but for Cain and his offering he had no regard" (Genesis 4:4-5). This divine snub sets the stage (however unjustifiably) for Cain's fratricide, yet the rabbis seek explanations of a different nature.[4]

The first rabbinic explanation is economic. Cain and Abel have divided the world between them, one brother claiming all the land, the other all the material possessions, and they proceed to fight over issues

[3] Genesis Rabbah 22, 5 (Teodor-Albeck edition, 213-14), with slight revisions.

[4] Perhaps the rabbis did not think the minor slight justified Cain's horrific response, or perhaps they assumed that God's explanation to Cain that his offering was rejected because of his behavior would have dissuaded Cain from killing his brother—had sacrifice been the issue. "The Lord said to Cain, 'Why are you angry, and why has your countenance fallen? If you do well, will you not be accepted?'" (Genesis 4:6-7).

of ownership. The second (offered by Rabbi Joshua of Sikhnin) involves the future glory of Israel: each brother wants the Temple to be built (millennia in the future, by a yet unestablished nation) in his territory. In support of this interpretation, Rabbi Joshua cites a biblical verse that likens Zion (i.e., Jerusalem, the site of the Temple) to a field: "Zion shall be ploughed like a field" (Micah 3:12). If so, goes the rabbinic logic, the biblical statement that the fratricide occurred "when they were in the field" (Genesis 4:8) is an oblique allusion to Jerusalem and the Temple, and thus a clue to Cain's motivation. Finally, Rav Huna argues that Cain and Abel fought over who will take Abel's twin sister for a wife. As readers familiar with Genesis will know, no twin sister has been mentioned at this point, nor any other daughter of Adam and Eve. But the Bible's silence on this point raises real difficulty since immediately after Cain is punished for his act, "Cain knew his wife, and she conceived and bore Enoch" (Genesis 4:17). When did this wife appear, and whence? Adam and Eve are the first human couple, and so far they have only had two sons.[5] Rav Huna is killing two birds with one stone: Adam and Eve must have had a daughter, explaining both how Cain could have a wife, and the roots of his dispute with Abel. (Incest is a disturbing but inevitable result of humanity having emerged from a single set of parents).

I cite this section of commentary because it exemplifies some of the key characteristics of rabbinic biblical interpretation, also known as midrash. Midrash is a conscious and deliberate engagement of Scripture, often responding to textual difficulties. At its best, it provides real insight into the biblical text, whether by connecting disparate biblical verses, calling attention to broader interpretive issues, or through other interpretive means. Midrash seeks to smooth out the rough spots in Scripture while encouraging us to read the Bible in a new light. Of course, most of this book has dealt with Springsteen's reworking of traditional religious themes and biblical motifs, and in that regard all of the lyrics discussed

[5] It is not until significantly later that we hear, in a passing remark, that daughters were born too: "The days of Adam after he became the father of Seth were eight hundred years; and he had other sons and daughters" (Genesis 5:4), daughters born too late to resolve the mystery of Cain's wife.

in this book are midrashic in some sense. What distinguishes the songs in this section is their explicit, sustained treatment of a biblical narrative, such that it becomes a key feature of the song's meaning.[6]

It merits mention that the phrase "Springsteen's midrash" openly rejects the notion that Springsteen's biblical references are vestigial traces of a Catholic childhood. I have critiqued Andrew Greeley's theory of Springsteen's Catholic "pre-conscious" in the introduction. But even Jim Cullen, whose analysis of the role of religion in Springsteen's music is, to my mind, more compelling, casts Springsteen primarily as a recipient of the views of earlier generations, calling the relevant chapter "Inherited Imagination." Cullen describes Springsteen "exploring old ideas and themes, adapting them reinvigorating them through the medium of popular culture," while I wish to focus on the more radical revisions I find in some of his works.[7]

"Swallowed Up (In the Belly of the Whale)" *(Wrecking Ball)*

The title of this song recalls the biblical story of Jonah, who was swallowed up by, and lived for three days within, a great fish, now universally referred to as a whale. The biblical story opens with God commanding the prophet Jonah to preach to the inhabitants of Nineveh, the great Assyrian capital located near modern-day Mosul, Iraq. But instead of obeying God's command, Jonah "set out to flee to Tarshish from the presence of the Lord. He went down to Joppa and found a ship going to Tarshish … away from the presence of the Lord" (Jonah 1:3).[8] This exchange is generally interpreted as an indication of Jonah's erroneous belief that God's dominion is geographically delimited and Tarshish lies beyond God's reach. But Jonah soon learns that God's presence extends far beyond the borders of ancient Israel, as the Lord sends a strong wind

[6] Some songs are on the borderline. The revision of Ezekiel's vision in "Devils & Dust" could have been discussed in this chapter, rather than chapter four.

[7] Cullen, *Born in the U.S.A.*, 162.

[8] The location of Tarshish is a matter of dispute. Ancient commentators identified it with Carthage (in modern-day Libya), while most modern authorities believe it is the ancient city of Tartessos, on the southern coast of Spain.

on the sea that threatens to break the ship. Jonah knows that the storm is his fault and volunteers himself as a sacrifice: "Pick me up and throw me into the sea … and it will become calm. I know that it is my fault that this great storm has come upon you" (Jonah 1:12). Though the sailors initially refuse, the violence of the storm ultimately causes them to relent and throw Jonah into the raging waters, and "the Lord provided a huge fish to swallow Jonah, and Jonah was in the belly of the fish three days and three nights" (Jonah 1:17). Jonah then prays to the Lord and repents his transgression, and so God commands the fish to vomit Jonah onto the shores of Nineveh. Jonah enters the great city, preaches repentance, and is able to sway the Ninevites from their sinful ways, and ultimately God "relented and did not bring on them the destruction he had threatened" (Jonah 3:10).

The story of Jonah has played a significant role in the liturgy of both the synagogue and the church, with each tradition emphasizing different aspects of the story. At least as far back as Babylonian Talmud (whose compilation began in the fourth century CE), the book of Jonah has been read in the synagogue on the afternoon of Yom Kippur, the Day of Atonement, with the atonement of Nineveh held up as a model of God's mercy. Prior to the liturgical reform of the Second Vatican Council in the early 1960s, the Roman Catholic Church incorporated parts of the book of Jonah into the liturgy of Holy Saturday, the day before Easter Sunday.[9] In the context of Holy Week, Jonah's disappearance into and subsequent reemergence from the belly of the fish "is an illustration of the death of the Messiah for sins not His own and of the Messiah's resurrection."[10] Though focused on different aspects of the book, both Jewish and Christian readers have traditionally emphasized two elements: God's unlimited reach, and the power of divine forgiveness. In "Swallowed Up (In the Belly of the Whale)," Springsteen offers a strong revisionist reading of the story of Jonah.

---

[9] That practice was discontinued after Vatican II, though the third chapter of Jonah is still read during Lent. See the summary in Jack M. Sasson, *The Anchor Bible: Jonah* (New York: Doubleday, 1990), 28-29.

[10] E. J. Young, *An Introduction to the Old Testament* (Grand Rapids, MI: Eerdmans, 1960), 263; cited in Sasson, *Jonah*, 324.

The song opens with an idyllic maritime scene: "I fell asleep on a dark and starless night, with nothing but the cloak of God's mercy over me." The opening differs from the scriptural narrative in two ways. First, Jonah takes to the sea as a way of escaping God's presence, while the sailor in "Swallowed Up (In the Belly of the Whale)" experiences God's protective mercy at sea. Second, Jonah also falls asleep at sea, but in a far less peaceful setting: "Then the mariners were afraid, and each cried to his god. They threw the cargo that was in the ship into the sea, to lighten it for them. Jonah, meanwhile, had gone down into the hold of the ship and had lain down, and was fast asleep" (Jonah 1:5). Jonah's sleep is clearly a defense mechanism of sorts, an internal analogue to his flight to Tarshish in an attempt to avoid God's assignment. At this point, the song breaks more sharply with the Book of Jonah. In his dream, the sailor comes upon a strange earth and a black cave, where "I dreamt I awoke, as if buried in my grave." In dreaming of his wakefulness the sailor realizes that he is living in a world without grace, where one who is swallowed up is not taken into God's mercy but rather disappears from the world; the great fish is not a vehicle of salvation but of destruction, its belly piled high with the bones of the sailors it devoured. This sight leads to a crisis of faith, as the singer laments the misguided faith humanity placed in itself and in God: "We trusted our skills and our good selves, put our faith that with God the righteous in this world prevail." Descent into the belly of the whale effectively reverses Jonah's experience. Jonah initially believes that he can flee God, but repents in the belly of the great fish and recognizes God's great mercy. The sailor in "Swallowed Up (In the Belly of the Whale)" begins cloaked in God's mercy, but after being swallowed by the whale, comes to believe that his faith is unfounded.

To this point, I have contrasted "Swallowed Up (In the Belly of the Whale)" with the traditional themes of the book of Jonah—repentance, divine forgiveness, renewal and resurrection. However, there is an aspect of the Jonah story that is much more congruent with Springsteen's dark vision. The third chapter of the book crowns the prophetic mission a success. In keeping with God's instructions, Jonah walks through the city of Nineveh announcing its imminent destruction, but "the people of Nineveh believed God; they proclaimed a fast, and everyone, great and small, put on sackcloth" (Jonah 3:5). The king of the city dons sackcloth as well, and orders a period of fast for all Ninevites, human and animal alike: "All shall turn from their evil ways and from the violence that is in their hands. Who knows? God may relent and change his mind; he may turn from his fierce anger, so that we do not perish" (Jonah 3:8-9). The fasting and supplication are efficacious and Nineveh is saved. "God changed his mind about the calamity that he had said he would bring upon them; and he did not do it" (Jonah 3:10).

But the book does not conclude here. The next chapter finds Jonah dejected and angry over the success of his mission:

> He prayed to the Lord and said, "O Lord! Is not this what I said while was still in my own country? That is why I fled to Tarshish at the beginning; for I knew that you are a gracious God and merciful ... And now, O Lord, please take my life from me, for it is better for me to die than to live." (Jonah 4:1-3)

This is a stunning development. Nineveh has repented, God mercifully spares the city, yet Jonah berates God for doing so. The different responses to Nineveh's repentance, God's acceptance versus Jonah's rejection, turn on different interpretations of Jonah's announcement that "forty days more, and Nineveh shall be overthrown!" (Jonah 3:4). Most readers of the Jonah story, both ancient and contemporary, have understood Jonah's words as a threat and thus an implicit call for repentance—if you do not repent, Nineveh will be overthrown. This is also how the men and women of Nineveh understood Jonah's words, as they immediately proclaimed a fast in the hope that "God may relent and change his mind" (Jonah 3:9). More significantly, God appears to have understood the message to Nineveh in these terms, for the city is, in fact, spared. Jonah alone understands his message as a factual declaration: "Nineveh *shall be* overthrown!" No ifs, ands, or buts.[11] When God spares the city, Jonah's prophecy (as he understands it) is confounded and, dismayed, he cites Nineveh's survival as the reason for his initial flight ("This is why I fled to Tarshish at the beginning")—not because he believed that God's dominion does not extend beyond the borders of ancient Israel, but rather because he knew "that you are a gracious God and merciful" (Jonah 4:2). Jonah did not doubt God's *ability* to destroy Nineveh, he doubted God's *resolve* to do so. Jonah fled to avoid having to prophesy the destruction of Nineveh, knowing that God might not follow through.

After the angry exchange with God, Jonah sets up a booth outside the city to see what will befall it. God initially provides Jonah with a shady bush for protection, but then sends a worm to attack and wilt the bush, leaving Jonah exposed to the sun. Jonah is angered by the loss of the bush and asks to die, but God responds: "You are concerned about the bush ... should I not be concerned about Nineveh, that great city, in which there are more than a hundred and twenty thousand people who do not know their right hand from their left, and also many animals?" (Jonah 4:10-11). These words, the book's last, are more suggestive than conclusive. If the phrase "who do not know their right hand from their left" refers to the moral confusion of Nineveh's residents, Jonah's distress becomes coherent. Even after fasting and praying, the people of Nineveh maintain their immoral behavior. But if the phrase means something else, Jonah's anger at God is utterly perplexing. On either interpretation, we find ourselves much closer to the tone and message of "Swallowed Up (In the Belly of the Whale)." The singer believed "that with God the righteous in this world prevail" but was disappointed; Jonah feared from the outset that God would allow the unrighteous to survive—and his fears were confirmed. Or perhaps the prophet sent to help save the people of Nineveh is shown to be a bloodthirsty character, eager to

---

[11] At the risk of veering too far into biblical philology, it merits mention that the Hebrew root *h.p.k*, translated *overthrown* above, can also mean "have a change of heart" or "repent." So while Jonah thinks he is prophesying the destruction of Nineveh ("the city will be overthrown"), his words can also refer to the city's repentance ("the city will repent"). For a discussion, see Sasson, *Jonah*, 234-5.

witness their death. Though their respective starting points and journeys are reversed (faith in God followed by a frightful descent into the whale versus conflict with God followed by a redemptive descent), the singer and Jonah ultimately arrive at a similar point. In this sense, "Swallowed Up (In the Belly of the Whale)" is not so much a revision of the book of Jonah as a dark mirror held up to it, making explicit the disturbing aspects of the biblical work that traditional readers have chosen to ignore.

"Into the Fire" *(The Rising)*

"Into the Fire," written in response to the attacks of 9/11, is narrated by a person trapped in a burning building, who witnesses a firefighter's efforts on behalf of others and his ultimate self-sacrifice.[12] My analysis focuses on two biblical motifs found in the song: the firefighter's ascent into the fire, and his laying on of hands on the singer. The first is expressed in the statement that the firefighter was called "someplace higher, somewhere up the stairs, into the fire." Rising into fire makes good sense as a depiction of the attack on the Twin Towers, but the firefighter is *called* someplace higher, not just physically higher, but to a spiritually elevated realm. As Springsteen writes: "Of the many tragic images of that day, the picture I couldn't let go of was of the emergency workers going up the stairs as others rushed down to safety. The sense of duty, the courage. Ascending into … what? The religious image of ascension."[13] But ascension into fire is not so common, as the notion that fire occupies a higher religious plane is at odds with the common identification of fire with hell and the netherworld. There is, however, one fiery ascent in the Hebrew Bible, namely, the account of the prophet Elijah's death, a narrative whose core themes resonate with "Into the Fire."

Elijah and Elisha, his disciple, are itinerant prophets who travel from one town to another, sometimes greeted by Elijah's local followers.

[12] On "Into the Fire" as part of *The Rising*'s poetic engagement with mourning, see Roxanne Harde, "'May Your Hope Give Us Hope': *The Rising* as a Site of Mourning," in Harde and Streight, *Reading the Boss*, 243-265.
[13] Springsteen, *Songs*, 304.

Knowing that his death is near, Elijah asks Elisha not to accompany him farther: "Stay here; for the Lord has sent me as far as Bethel" (2 Kings 2:2). But Elisha refuses to leave his master. "As the Lord lives, and as you yourself live, I will not leave you" (2 Kings 2:2), he says, so the two proceed together to Bethel. There they are greeted by a company of local prophets who know of Elijah's imminent death, and ask Elisha if he is aware that this is the day God will take his master away. But Elisha is too pained to speak of the topic, saying only "Yes, I know; keep silent" (2 Kings 2:3). Elijah receives new instructions from God—he is to proceed to Jericho, so again Elijah asks Elisha to remain behind, and Elisha repeats his answer, "as the Lord lives and as you yourself live, I will not leave you" (2 Kings 2:4). Upon their arrival at Jericho, a local group of prophets confronts Elisha with the same question about his master's imminent death, and he says, "I know; be silent" (2 Kings 2:5). After God directs Elijah to proceed to the Jordan River, Elijah tries a third time to spare Elisha the sight of his death, asking him to remain behind, and for a third time Elisha refuses: "As the Lord lives, and as you yourself live, I will not leave you" (2 Kings 2:6). So the two walk to the Jordan River as a large company of prophets bears witness from a distance and, upon reaching the river, "Elijah took his mantle and rolled it up, and struck the water; the water was parted to the one side and to the other, until the two of them crossed on dry ground" (2 Kings 2:8). Knowing these are their final moments together, Elijah asks what he may do for Elisha and Elisha asks to be recognized as Elijah's chief prophetic heir. However, this is a matter of divine inspiration that Elijah cannot grant. All he can tell Elisha is that "if you see me as I am being taken from you, it will be granted you; if not, it will not" (2 Kings 2:10). As the two walk along together,

> a chariot of fire and horses of fire separated the two of them, and Elijah ascended in a whirlwind into heaven. Elisha kept watching and crying out "Father, father! The chariots of Israel and its horsemen!" But when he could no longer see him, he

> grasped his own clothes and tore them in two pieces. (2 Kings 2:11-12)

The beauty of this narrative ought be savored. On the one hand, Elijah's desire to spare his disciple the pain of witnessing his death, and his entreaties that Elisha remain behind. On the other hand, Elisha's resolve to remain by his master's side, even though it pains him beyond words. Elisha's exclamation "the chariots of Israel and its horsemen" (2 Kings 2:12) indicates that he does indeed see the chariot of fire, and that God has granted Elisha's request to be recognized as Elijah's chief disciple.

The image of fiery ascent in "Into the Fire" creates a dialogue with the key motifs of its biblical precedent, the Elijah narrative: the pain of a loved one's death, the desire to remain with them as long as possible, and the survivors' hope to prove worthy successors to the departed loved one. Elisha cannot prevent the death of his beloved teacher, but he can preserve Elijah's prophetic mission, a point the Bible highlights in a number of ways. After Elijah is taken to heaven, Elisha, who had torn his own cloak in a sign of mourning, "took the mantle of Elijah that had fallen from him, and struck the water … [and] the water was parted to one side and to the other, and Elisha went over" (2 Kings 2:14). Elisha thus assumes the mantle of his master, and replicates Elijah's miraculous splitting of the Jordan and, in later narratives, other miracles as well.[14]

These motifs are buttressed by a second, closely related, biblical theme, namely, the laying on of hands. After the firefighter draws the singer out of the darkness, "you held me in the light you gave, you lay your hand on me, then walked into the silence of your smoky grave." Laying on of hands is a biblical ritual that serves in both the Hebrew Bible and the New Testament to transfer inspiration and inspired authority. As Moses approaches his death, God commands him to "'take Joshua son of Nun, a

[14] Elisha increases the bread and oil of a poor woman (2 Kings 4:4-7), replicating Elijah's miracle in 1 Kings 17:8-16; Elisha resurrects the son of the Shunammite woman (2 Kings 4:32-37), replicating Elijah's actions in 1 Kings 17:17-24. Incidentally, the story of Elisha's discipleship is the source of the English idiom "to assume the mantle," meaning to take on the responsibilities of a particular office.

man in whom is the spirit, and lay your hand upon him' … So Moses did as the Lord commanded him … he laid his hands on him and commissioned him" (Numbers 27:18-23). The book of Deuteronomy confirms the significance of the ritual when it states that "Joshua son of Nun was full of the spirit of wisdom, because Moses had laid his hands on him; and the Israelites obeyed him" (Deuteronomy 34:9). In the New Testament, laying on of hands transfers the divine spirit from Peter and John to a group of Samaritan believers who had recently been baptized in the name of Christ: "The two went down and prayed for them that they might receive the Holy Spirit … Then Peter and John laid their hands on them, and they received the Holy Spirit" (Acts 8:15-17). In laying his hands on the singer just prior to his death, the firefighter indicates his desire to bequeath his spirit to him, almost commissioning the singer as an heir. At this point the two biblical motifs converge. Elisha's wish to be a worthy successor and the laying on of hands as a transfer of inspiration both entails the imminent death of a leader and bespeaks the hope to be worthy successors. And this is precisely the hope of "Into the Fire," as the song's chorus clearly states:

> May your strength give us strength
> May your faith give us faith
> May your hope give us hope
> May your love give us love

Like Elisha, Joshua, and anyone who has received the grace of another, the singer hopes to be deserving of the gift, and prays that we prove ourselves worthy heirs to those who made the ultimate sacrifice. By alluding to Elijah's ascent and the biblical laying on of hands, "Into the Fire" transforms loss into a moment of potential inspiration.[15] The fireman's death is not inherently redemptive—he saves but is not a savior; his death will only be transformed into a redemptive act if it inspires strength, love, faith, and hope in others.

---

[15] It is interesting that "Into the Fire" deals with these issues with minimal martyrological imagery. The phrase "you … lay your young body down" could have been the basis for a fuller martyrological representation, but the song does not develop in that direction.

"Adam Raised a Cain" *(Darkness on the Edge of Town)*

"Adam Raised a Cain" recounts a son's tumultuous relationship with his father, his departure from home, eventual return, and ongoing struggle to find peace with the fact that he is his father's son. The song addresses a number of familiar Springsteen themes: the alienation between son and father ("My Father's House"), the deadening effect of labor ("Factory," "The Promised Land"), and the desire to break free of one's hometown (much of *Born to Run*). "Adam Raised a Cain" interweaves two biblical threads into its treatment of these themes. One, a midrash on the horrifying Cain and Abel narrative. Another, a fascinating critique of the Christian doctrine of original sin.

Adam raised a Cain is plainly a reference to the Genesis account of the first family, but it is a perplexing one. The first chapters of Genesis are generally understood to contain two discrete narratives, one dealing with Adam and Eve, their disobedience, and the subsequent punishment; the other with Cain and Abel, their conflict, and Cain's fratricide. The song's brief synopsis of the latter events ("In the Bible Cain slew Abel and East of Eden he was cast") makes no mention of Adam. But a moment's reflection suffices to recognize how problematic it is that Adam and Eve are isolated from the story of Cain and Abel. Adam and Eve are the two brothers' parents—the first human parents raising the first human children. The phrase "Adam raised a Cain" reintroduces Adam into the narrative, identifying him as the first man charged with guiding his sons into manhood, and also the first to fail.

"Adam Raised a Cain," then, presses us to consider the unacknowledged generational dynamic at work in the Bible's first murder, and, further, to meditate on the tragic dysfunction of the primordial family—all of which serves as the backdrop to the singer's tense relationship with his own father. The singer drives this point home by punctuating key moments in the song with the phrase "Adam raised a Cain": after the fight that leads to the singer's departure from his home; when the singer returns home but remains a stranger to his own family; and when the son recognizes he has received his father's vices ("you inherit the sins, you inherit the flames, Adam raised a Cain"). The repeated invocation of Genesis 4 suggests the tensions between the singer and his father are structural, reaching back to the very dawn of humanity. At the same time, the song argues that present-day paternal dysfunction illuminates the Genesis narrative, reintroducing Adam into the story of Cain and Abel. This approach calls attention to, and offers a corrective for, the curious dissociation of Adam and Eve from the Cain and Abel narrative. Adam sired and raised a fratricide and is undoubtedly implicated in that tragedy.

A second, less obvious theological strand is introduced in the statements "you're born into this life paying for the sins of somebody else's past," and "you inherit the sins, you inherit the flames." The assertion that one is born bearing the sins of others is nothing other than the doctrine of original sin, according to which Adam and Eve's transgression in the Garden of Eden has been transmitted, through the sexual nature of procreation, to all humanity, so that every person is born already in a state of sin. This doctrine is not found in the book of Genesis. Adam and Eve's transgression is linked to sexual self-awareness, since no sooner had they eaten the forbidden fruit than "the eyes of both were opened, and they knew that they were naked" (Genesis 3:7). But this is a far cry from the idea that sexual reproduction results in sin permeating human existence. God's command to Adam and Eve to "be fruitful and multiply, and fill the earth and subdue it" (Genesis 1:28)—a command that precedes the Fall—indicates that sexual reproduction was present even in humanity's prelapsarian state, so while the fruit of the Tree of Knowledge causes Adam and Eve to feel shame, it does not introduce a new reality. Moreover, God metes out punishment that extends to all generations following the transgression, but not in the form of original sin. To Eve, pain of childbearing and sexual dominance of her husband; to Adam, the need to toil for food (Genesis 3:16-17).

Looking beyond Genesis, we find the doctrine of original sin is not attested in the Hebrew Bible,[16] and appears to be inspired by (rather

[16] "It is to be concluded, therefore, that the Old Testament books supply no evidence of a doctrine of the Fall having been extracted out of Genesis," Frederick Robert Tennant, *The Sources of the Doctrines of the Fall and Original Sin* (New York: Schocken, 1968), 94.

than formulated in) key Pauline passages, most notably Romans 5. There Paul draws a direct line between Adam's sin and the universal presence of sin in the world—"therefore, just as sin came into the world through one man, and death came through sin, and so death spread to all because all have sinned" (Romans 5:12). But Paul teaches that Adam's sin paves the way for the (plural) sins of those who follow him, not for a universal sinfulness shared by all. Paul also does not tie Adam's sin to sexual desire (either as the result of the sin or as the means of its transmission), but rather to disobedience of God's command ("For just as by the one man's disobedience the many were made sinners, so by the one man's obedience the many will be made righteous" [Romans 5:19]). But while Paul's verses do not contain the doctrine of original sin, they play a prominent role in the discussion of later Church Fathers who contributed to the formulation of this doctrine, that was to find its mature expression in the work of St. Augustine.[17]

Though the history of the doctrine of original sin lies beyond the purview of the present discussion, it is significant that it came to be closely linked with baptism. For while ritual immersion is amply attested in the New Testament and regularly referred to in terms of "remission of sins," the idea that baptism counteracts original sin was still being argued by Augustine himself.[18] As Pier Franco Beatrice writes, "Augustine stands firm in maintaining that the ills with which babies are afflicted [and to which infant baptism responds, AYI] can only be viewed as the just punishment, imposed on them by God, for the original sin contracted from Adam."[19] Like so much of Augustine's teachings, this view of baptism has become authoritative Christian doctrine.

---

[17] See the survey of patristic authors before Augustine in Tennant, *The Sources and Doctrines*, 273-345; on Augustine's decisive influence on the crystallization of the doctrine, and the historical and theological implications of his position, see Pier Franco Beatrice, *The Transmission of Sin: Augustine and Pre-Augustine Sources*, translated by Adam Kamesar (Oxford and New York: Oxford University Press, 2013).

[18] See the extensive survey in Lars Hartman, "*Into the Name of the Lord Jesus*": *Baptism in the Early Church* (Edinburgh: T&T Clark, 1997). None of the passages Hartman discusses speak of the doctrine of original sin.

[19] Beatrice, *The Transmission of Sin*, 79.

Why does Springsteen invoke the doctrine of original sin in a song about Adam and Cain, when this teaching has traditionally been associated with Adam and Eve? Because, at its core, "Adam Raised a Cain" seeks to revise the current understanding of original sin. While it is true that "you're born into this life paying for the sins of somebody else's past," the sins in question do not originate with Adam and Eve, are not transmitted sexually, and are not remitted through baptism. This last point explains the song's opening lines: "In the summer that I was baptized, my father held me to his side, as they put me to the water, he said how on that day I cried." Though baptized, the singer pays for someone else's sins all the same. "Adam Raised a Cain" argues, in effect, that baptism cannot absolve because it does not address the true sin that passes from one generation to the next, namely, the father's mistreatment of his son, and the anger and frustration thus bequeathed.

Springsteen does not specify the father's actions, but the song's title may offer a clue. "Adam raised a Cain" is grammatically incorrect: the indefinite article *a* can introduce an indefinite subject ("Adam raised a great kid"), but not a proper noun. Any competent English speaker will recognize "I had lunch with *a* Jim" as a mistake. Why, then, does Springsteen title the song "Adam Raised *a* Cain" rather than "Adam Raised Cain"?[20] Because the error draws our attention to the possibility of replacing *Cain* with its (grammatically correct) homonym, *cane*. Adam raised a cane: the father beat his son.[21] This, the song tells us, is the true original sin passed from one generation to the next. Adam and Eve are not the axis that transmits sin. It passes from Adam to Cain, fathers and sons in an endless chain of anger and violence—sins that baptism cannot absolve.

"Jesus Was an Only Son" *(Devils & Dust)*

In this beautiful song, Springsteen engages the Passion narrative, the apex of the gospel account of Jesus' life and death and one of the key

[20] In addition to grammatical correctness, the omission of the indefinite article ("raised Cain" instead of "raised a Cain") would have echoed the idiom "raising Cain," meaning to behave in an unruly or disruptive manner.

[21] The motif of paternal abuse is also intimated in the lines "Daddy worked his whole life for nothing but the pain, now he walks these empty rooms looking for something to blame."

moments in Christian theology. At first glance, the phrase "Jesus was an only son" is a familiar trope, arguably a cliché.[22] Jesus' sonship is a common theme in the Gospels. Jesus speaks of himself in these terms when he famously proclaims that "all things have been committed to me by my Father. No one knows the Son except the Father, and no one knows the Father except the Son and those to whom the Son chooses to reveal him" (Matthew 11:27); a heavenly voice affirms Jesus' status as God's son when, following Jesus's baptism, proclaiming, "this is my Son, the Beloved, with whom I am well pleased" (Matthew 3:17); and the Gospel of John famously characterizes Jesus as God's only son: "For God so loved the world, that he gave his only Son, that whoever believes in him should not perish but have eternal life" (John 3:16).

These passages, and others like them, create the expectation that "Jesus was an only son" will invoke Jesus' relationship with God, but this expectation is immediately thwarted: "Jesus was an only son as he walked up Calvary Hill, his mother Mary walking beside him, in the path where his blood spilled." The song refers to Jesus as Mary's son, not God's, a shift that disrupts the traditional understanding of the song's title, and introduces a counternarrative that focuses on the humanity of Jesus' life rather than its divinity. As part of this shift, Springsteen's interpretation highlights the role of Jesus' earthly mother and the absence of his heavenly father. For it was Mary, the song reminds us, that stood by Jesus in his final hours, walking through his spilled blood to remain by his side. It was also Mary who cared for Jesus as he was growing up: "Jesus was an only son in the hills of Nazareth, as he lay reading the Psalms of David at his mother's feet." The scene is one of loving intimacy between Jesus and his mother, that emphasizes Mary's status as the parent for whom Jesus is the only son, her steadfast presence by Jesus' side casting into sharp relief God's—the father's—absence.

---

[22] The claim that Jesus was an only child is not historically true: James, the brother of the Lord, was an important figure among Jesus' early followers, on whom see John Painter, *Just James: The Brother of Jesus in History and Tradition* (Minneapolis: Fortress, 1999). As with other religious statements Springsteen employs in his writing, historical accuracy is less important to my analysis than their traditional understanding.

The second stanza sets aside the Gospel narrative and turns to motherhood more broadly, portraying mothers promising their sleeping children that "I'll be by your side" and their prayer "that no shadow, no darkness, no tolling bell, shall pierce your dreams this night." The image of maternal care is touching but, for Mary and Jesus, especially poignant. For uniquely among all mothers, Mary's prayers for her son's well-being were addressed to her son's father; every other mother prays to God to protect her child, Mary prays to God to protect *their* child. But the listener knows what Mary does not as she sits by her sleeping infant son: her prayers will not be answered, and she will watch her son die an excruciating death. Her promise "I'll be by your side" is fulfilled in the previous stanza's description of Mary "walking beside [Jesus], in the path where his blood spilled," but not in the manner she intended. She prays that no darkness "pierce your dreams," but will eventually watch as Roman soldiers "came to Jesus and saw that he was already dead … [and] one of the soldiers pierced his side with a spear" (John 19:33-34). Without mentioning the holy family explicitly, the second stanza further contrasts maternal presence and paternal absence, as Jesus' heavenly father ignores Mary's prayers and fails to fulfill the most basic parental obligation, to protect his child from harm.

The contrast between Mary and God corresponds to the core theological tension between Jesus' humanity and his divinity, and the song's stress on Mary's role is framed by its broader emphasis on Jesus' humanity. The third stanza returns to the Gospel narrative, portraying the night before the crucifixion, when Jesus prays at Gethsemane: "My Father, if it is possible, let this cup pass from me; yet not what I want but what you want" (Matthew. 26:39). Springsteen renders this moment thus: "In the garden at Gethsemane, he prayed for the life he'd never live, he beseeched his Heavenly Father to remove the cup of death from his lips."[23] Springsteen focuses here on one of Jesus' most

[23] The Gospel of Matthew has Jesus asking God to pass "this cup" from him, a phrase generally linked to the Hebrew Bible's association of God's cup with punishment: "Stand up, O Jerusalem, you who have drunk at the hand of the Lord the cup of his wrath" (Isaiah 51:17); "For thus says the Lord: If those who do not deserve to drink the cup still have to drink it, shall you be the one to go unpunished? You shall not go unpunished; you must drink it" (Jeremiah 49:12). Springsteen's phrase "cup of death," then, accords with the traditional understanding of the phrase.

"human" moments, a moment that maintains an uneasy relationship with the passages in which Jesus foretells his death and resurrection. Consider Matthew 16: "From that time Jesus began to show his disciples that he must go to Jerusalem and suffer many things from the elders and chief priests and scribes, and be killed, and on the third day be raised" (Matthew 16:21). When Peter expresses his hope that no harm befall his teacher Jesus says to him, "Get behind me, Satan! You are a stumbling block to me" (v. 23). Jesus knows that he will die and embraces that fate. Indeed, Jesus' death and subsequent resurrection are the theological culmination of the Gospels. Why, then, on the night before his crucifixion, does he pray that the cup of death "pass from me"? Whatever the precise meaning of Jesus' lament over "the life he'd never live," Springsteen draws attention to a New Testament episode that highlights Jesus' humanity and the draw earthly life held for him. But as with Mary's prayer for her sleeping infant's wellbeing, God refuses Jesus' request and allows his son to die.

The fourth stanza speaks of this death as "a loss that can never be replaced … A light you'll never find in another's face." Here again, the song is at odds with the traditional understanding of Jesus' death as a prelude to the triumph of his resurrection. "Death where is your sting?" Paul asks (1 Corinthians 15:55-56), for Jesus' death is not permanent and can be overcome. But "Jesus Was an Only Son" is concerned with Jesus the man whose loss will be forever mourned by his mother and by the men and women who loved him. In the song's concluding lines, Jesus kisses his grieving mother's hands and asks that she still her tears since "the soul of the universe willed a world and it appeared." Jesus' detached, theological language draws a sharp contrast between his relationship with each of his parents. The physical tenderness and emotional intimacy he shares with his mother, on the one hand, and his distance from his father, to whom he refers as "the soul of the universe" rather than, simply, "my Father."

Springsteen's portrait of Jesus does not openly contradict the Gospels, as they too depict him as a man who grows up by his mother's side and prays for his life at Gethsemane. But "Jesus Was an Only Son" offers an untraditional portrait in the way that it highlights Jesus' humanity, Mary's constant maternal presence, and God's paternal absence. In so doing, Springsteen's powerful midrash recaptures both the poignancy and the profound humanity of Jesus' life and death.

Conclusion

This book remains, in one sense, unfinished. From the boy prophet of "The E Street Shuffle" (*The Wild, the Innocent & the E Street Shuffle*), through the titular "Soul Driver" (*Human Touch*), and from "Bishop Danced" (*Tracks*) to "Countin' on a Miracle" (*The Rising*), many other Bruce Springsteen songs touch on religious themes. However, my goal is not to catalogue every biblical and theological reference in Springsteen's songbook. It is, rather, to chart the decades-long artistic relationship Springsteen has maintained with traditional religious sources and themes, and to flesh out the dramatic shifts in his approach over the years. The fierce anti-religious imagery of "Lost in the Flood" has little in common with "Higher Ground," nor the depravity of "Nebraska" with the grace of "Kingdom of Days."[1] My goal, in other words, has been

[1] Springsteen himself appears to have repented some of his extreme anti-church pronouncements early on. While writing this book, I received an email from Ned Pelger, a roadie on Springsteen's 1978 *Darkness on the Edge of Town* tour, who writes: "We were in Pittsburg at a small venue (the first half of the tour played small venues, then Bruce's popularity exploded and we went to arenas). Every show I would walk with Bruce and the mixer to make sure every seat had good sound. Bruce was talking about getting a note from someone whose buddy just died in a motorcycle accident and wanted him to play 'Lost in the Flood.' It wasn't on the set list and Bruce had to work through the song to remember it. He kind of mumbled that he was embarrassed

to demonstrate the existence of a theological dimension in Springsteen's work, and to argue that we ought conceive of this dimension in the plural form, not as Springsteen's theology, but rather as his theologies.

Throughout the book, I have kept discussion of Springsteen the man to a minimum, focusing instead on his lyrics. Now that my analysis is complete, however, it is clear that the portrait that has emerged is very much at odds with Springsteen's popular image, perhaps to the point where the disparity will call the viability of my interpretation into question in the minds of some readers. Surely, one might object, we are not to think of Springsteen as some theological scholar or crypto-midrashist. This is, after all, rock 'n' roll. Fortunately, my argument does not require that we think of Springsteen in those terms.

Springsteen has characterized himself as an instinctive composer: "Whatever I hear, I digest very quickly, and it comes back out the way I want it to."[2] The process is not intellectual; Springsteen does not analyze the music he hears, so much as absorb and then employ it for his own musical purposes. It is the task of the musicologist to provide a detailed scholarly analysis of the result. A similar dynamic appears to be at work in his writing. In *Storytellers*, Springsteen provides an interpretation of "Devils and Dust" at the end of which he offers the audience a glimpse into this process: "How much of this was I thinking about when I wrote this song? None of it. How much of that was I feeling when I wrote this song? All of it."[3] The writing process, on Springsteen's testimony, is intuitive, "like a second language that you speak without thinking."[4] If we accept Springsteen's account of this process,[5] his public image

---

about some of the lyrics. The sound mixer asked why and Bruce explained that the 'nuns run bald through Vatican Halls pregnant, pleading immaculate conception' was embarrassing now. When he did the song, he just mumbled through those lines. By the way, he dedicated the song to the guy who died and it was one of the most moving songs I've ever heard." My thanks to Ned Pelger for his fascinating email.

[2] Chris Phillips, "*Born to Run*: The Lost Interviews: Part One," *Backstreets* 57 (1997); reprinted in Phillips and Masur, *Talk About a Dream*, 34.

[3] *Storytellers*, at the 12 minute mark.

[4] *Storytellers*, at the 1 hour and 19 minute mark.

[5] Though I do not consider Springsteen's interpretation of his songs authoritative (they are public documents that can be analyzed by a range of readers), an artist's songwriting process is inescapably internal, and he is the best and most reliable witness to it.

and the portrait that emerges from this book are easily reconciled. Simply stated, the biblical and theological themes in Springsteen's songs are elements—alongside memories, thoughts, imaginings—that he has assimilated in his mind and artistically reworked in his lyrics. The critical engagement of ancient sources, the transposition of transcendent motifs into a this-worldly key, the midrashic reinterpretations of the Bible, all these are more the result of intuitive artistry than bookish erudition. As with the musical aspect of his songs, the full (or at least fuller) meaning of Springsteen's lyrics comes to light through later reflection. And so, it falls to the scholar of Scripture and theology to provide an account of the ways Springsteen has woven these elements into his work, thereby revealing a heretofore unappreciated dimension of his artistry.

Acknowledgments

This book is a departure for me. My academic affiliation is with Rutgers' Department of Jewish Studies, where I teach rabbinic literature, the Dead Sea Scrolls, and medieval Jewish philosophy, and with the Department of Classics, where I focus on Plato. I do, however, have a long-standing interest in the encounter between ancient traditions and modern interpreters, particularly the ways sacred or canonic texts inform non-traditional writers. This interest gave rise to several academic studies,[1] as well as a more popular study of Hadag Nahash, an Israeli hip-hop band, and its innovative use

[1] See, for example, my analysis of Hebrew poet H. N. Bialik's use of biblical verses in the service of his Nietzschean characterization of poetic language in "Web of Chaos: Bialik and Nietzsche on Language, Truth and the Death of God," *Prooftexts* 21 (2001), 179-203; the theological underpinnings of Martin Heidegger's Kant essay in "The Creaturely Limits of Knowledge: Martin Heidegger's Theological Critique of Immanuel Kant," in Leonard V. Kaplan and Rudy Koshar, editors, *The Weimar Moment: Political Theology, Liberalism, and the Law* (Lanham, MD: Lexington Books, 2012), 123-144 (co-authored with Sam Moyn); and the ideological reworking of biblical and rabbinic terms in modern Hebrew in "Blorit: Pagan Mohawk or Sabra Forelock?: Ideologically Manipulative Secularization of Hebrew Terms in Socialist Zionist Israel," in Tope Omoniyi, editor, *The Sociology of Language and Religion: Change, Conflict, and Accommodation* (London and New York: Palgrave Macmillan, 2009), 84-124 (co-authored with Ghil'ad Zuckermann).

of phrases drawn from the Hebrew Bible and rabbinic sources.[2] After publishing the latter essay, I began to wonder if similar analysis would prove fruitful for American singers, and my thoughts gravitated toward Bruce Springsteen, a writer whose lyrics I knew contained religious terms and imagery. Of course, I could not propose such a course through either Jewish Studies or Classics, but Rutgers' Byrne Freshmen Seminars afforded me the freedom to teach material that lay outside the scope of my regular curricular offerings. After determining that Springsteen's lyrics provide sufficient material for a seminar, I taught "Bruce Springsteen's Theologies" in the Fall of 2013. Over the course of the semester, I realized that many Springsteen songs incorporated biblical themes in ways that were more subtle and more complex than I had initially recognized, and the exploration of this complexity ultimately resulted in this book. My first debt of gratitude, then, is to the Byrne Seminars—to Dr. Angela Mullis, the program director, and to the students who read and discussed Springsteen's lyrics with me. Byrne funds also allowed me to hire Joe Duncan as a research assistant in the summer of 2014, and I want to acknowledge this support and thank Joe for his help. Other Rutgers students have provided assistance with various aspects of this project, and I thank Isaac Woodward, Joshua Blachorsky, William Chen, and Antoinette Armocida.

Eileen Chapman, director of the Bruce Springsteen Special Collection housed at Monmouth University, generously provided me with articles and studies, including several that I could not otherwise have acquired. Melanie Paggioli invited me to speak at a conference organized by the Friends of the Bruce Springsteen Special Collection at Monmouth University in honor of Springsteen's 65th birthday, and it was there that I first presented my argument to colleagues. Thanks to Shawn Poole, who organized the sessions, and to the panelists and audience members who offered incisive comments. Linda Randall, in particular, provided helpful advice. Bill Wolff of Rowan University commented on the introduction.

[2] "A Measure of Beauty," *Jewish Review of Books* 3 (Fall 2010), 44-45. All of my academic publications are posted on Academia.edu.

My greatest debt is to my colleagues who read my earlier drafts of the entire manuscript and offered their comments and suggestions. Paul Contino of Pepperdine University offered insightful comments; Jonathan Cohen of the University of Virginia provided shared his extensive knowledge of Springsteen's corpus and of the scholarship it has engendered; Dr. Gayle Lasater Pagnoni brought her expertise as a scholar of American religion to bear on the manuscript; Benjamin Sommer of the Jewish Theological Seminary—Hebrew Bible scholar, Jewish theologian, and dedicated Springsteen fan—provided wonderfully attentive comments. An unanticipated benefit of this project was that it introduced me to my Rutgers colleague Lou Masur, author of *Runaway Dream:* Born to Run *and Bruce Springsteen's American Vision*. Lou read the manuscript and offered his observations along with greatly-appreciated advice and encouragement. In the last stages of my work, Abbie Reardon, a Rutgers doctoral student in English literature, commented perceptively on the structure and argument of the manuscript. Outside of academia, George Morga has been engaged in this project from its earliest stages, and has freely given of his encyclopedic knowledge of the New Jersey music scene, and Lou Pagnoni read the manuscript and valued encouragement. Jeff Pusar contributed to the project in his usual ways. I am profoundly grateful to all for their support and generosity.

Heartfelt thanks to Oliver L'eroe, for granting me permission to use his stunning photograph as the cover image. The picture beautifully captures the somber and contemplative tone of this study. Oliver's work can be found at: http://www.leroe24fotos.com. Anna Dorfman created the breathtaking cover design; a sample of the book covers she has designed is available here: http://www.annadorfman.com/.

Thanks to my family, and particularly to my father-in-law, David Surowitz, for suggesting I turn my Springsteen class into a book. To my wife, Hilit, and to our children—those in college, those in diapers, and those in between—endless love and gratitude.

Growing up in Cleveland Heights in the early 1980's, it was an unwritten law that the radio was to be tuned to WMMS on Friday evenings, when Kid Leo ended his Friday shift with "Born to Run," making it (along with Ian Hunter's "Cleveland Rocks," which followed immediately) the unofficial anthem of the weekend. Much has changed in the decades since I graduated high school and left Cleveland Heights. In the course of writing this book, I have often found myself thinking back on those days with great joy.

Springsteen's Cited Discography and Videography

Studio Albums

Greetings from Asbury Park, N.J. (1973)
The Wild, the Innocent & the E Street Shuffle (1973)
Born to Run (1975)
Darkness on the Edge of Town (1978)
The River (1980)
Nebraska (1982)
Born in the U.S.A. (1984)
Tunnel of Love (1987)
Human Touch (1992)
Lucky Town (1992)
The Ghost of Tom Joad (1995)
The Rising (2002)
Devils & Dust (2005)
Magic (2007)
Working on a Dream (2009)
Wrecking Ball (2012)
High Hopes (2014)

Live Albums

Live in Dublin (2007)

Compilation Albums

Tracks (1998)
The Promise (2010)

Videos

Bruce Springsteen: VH1 Storytellers. Directed by Dave Diomedi. Rutherford, NJ: Sony Legacy, 2005. DVD.

The Promise: The Making of Darkness on the Edge of Town. Directed by Thom Zimny. Colts Neck, NJ: Thrill Hill Productions, 2010. DVD.

Bibliography

Abrams, M. H. *Natural Supernaturalism: Tradition and Revolution in Romantic Literature*. New York: Norton, 1971.

Allen, Spencer L. "Mary Queen of Arkansas; Mary Queen of Heaven." Paper presented at *Glory Days: A Bruce Springsteen Symposium, Sept. 9th-11th, 2005*. West Long Beach, NJ.

Allison, Jr, Dale C., Jr. *The Intertextual Jesus: Scripture in Q*. Harrisburg, PA: Trinity International, 2000.

Arnoff, Stephen Hazan. "A Covenant Reversed: Bruce Springsteen and the Promised Land." In Harde and Streight, *Reading the Boss*, 177-200.

Auerbach, Erich. *Mimesis: The Representation of Reality in Western Literature*. Translated by Willard Trask. Princeton: Princeton University Press, 1953.

Augustine of Hippo. *The Confessions of Saint Augustine*. Translated by John K. Ryan. New York: Doubleday, 1988.

Balfour, Ian. *The Rhetoric of Romantic Prophecy*. Stanford, CA: Stanford University Press, 2002.

Beatrice, Pier Franco. *The Transmission of Sin: Augustine and Pre-Augustine Sources*. Translated by Adam Kamesar. Oxford and New York: Oxford University Press, 2013.

Bellamy, Brent. "Tear into the Guts: Whitman, Steinbeck, and the Durability of Lost Souls on the Road." *Canadian Review of American Studies/Revue canadienne d'études américaines* 41 (2011): 223-243.

Brown, Colin. *Christianity and Western Thought: A History of Philosophers, Ideas and Movements*. 2 Vols. Downers Grove, IL: Inter-Varsity, 2010.

Brown, David. *God and Grace of Body: Sacrament in Ordinary*. Oxford: Oxford University Press, 2007.

Brown, Raymond E. *The Virginal Conception and Bodily Resurrection of Jesus*. New York: Paulist, 1973.

Bryan, Christopher. *The Resurrection of the Messiah*. New York and Oxford: Oxford University Press, 2011.

Bühler, Pierre. "Tertullian: The Teacher of the *credo quia absurdum*." *Kierkegaard and the Patristic and Medieval Traditions*. Edited by Jon Stewart. Burlington, VT: Ashgate, 2008. 131-142.

Burger, Jeff. *Springsteen on Springsteen: Interviews, Speeches, and Encounters*. Chicago: Chicago Review, 2013.

Cavicchi, Daniel. *Tramps Like Us: Music and Meaning among Springsteen Fans*. New York and Oxford: Oxford University Press, 1998.

Cohen, Jonathan D. "'Can Music Save Your Mortal Soul?': Assessing Scholarship Concerning the Rock-Religion Phenomenon." Unpublished paper, 2013.

Collins, John J. "Apocalyptic Eschatology in the Ancient World." *The Oxford Handbook of Eschatology*. Edited by Jerry L. Walls. Oxford and New York: Oxford University Press, 2008. 40-55.

Contino, Paul. "The Theology of St. Augustine and Bruce Springsteen: 'Everybody's Got a Hungry Heart'." Villanova University. 29 Oct. 2009. Unpublished talk.

Corcoran, Neil. "Death's Honesty." "*Do You, Mr. Jones?" Bob Dylan with the Poets and the Professors*. Edited by Neil Corcoran. London: Chatto & Windus, 2002. 143-174.

Corn, David. "Bruce Springsteen Tells the Story of the Secret America." *Mother Jones* March, 1996. Reprinted in Burger, *Springsteen on Springsteen*, 213-217.

Costello, Elvis. Interview with Bruce Springsteen. *Spectacle: Elvis Costello with....* Sundance Channel, United Kingdom.; 20 January, 2010. Television. Reprinted in Philips and Masur, *Talk about a Dream*, 365-384.

Cowie, Jefferson R., and Lauren Boehm. "Dead Man's Town: 'Born In The U.S.A.,' Social History, And Working-Class Identity." *American Quarterly* 58 (2006): 353-78.

Craig, William Lane. *Time and Eternity: Exploring God's Relationship to Time.* Wheaton, IL: Crossway, 2001.

Cucciniello, Lisa. "Rose to Rosary: The Flower of Venus in Catholicism." *Rose Lore: Essays in Cultural History and Semiotics*. Edited by Frankie Hutton. Lanham, MD: Lexington, 2008. 63-91.

Cullen, Jim. *Born in the U.S.A.: Bruce Springsteen and the American Tradition.* Middletown, CT: Wesleyan University Press, 2005.

Detweiler, Craig. *A Matrix of Meanings: Finding God in Pop Culture*. Grand Rapids, MI: Baker Academic, 2003.

Diemling, Maria. "American Midrash: Biblical Motifs in the Work of Bruce Springsteen." *Retelling the Bible: Literary, Historical, and Social Contexts. Edited by* Lucie Dolezalová and Tamás Visi. Frankfurt/Main: Peter Lang, 2011. 355-368.

DiMartino, Dave. "Bruce Springsteen Takes It to the River." *Creem* January, 1981. Reprinted in Burger, *Springsteen on Springsteen*, 107-121.

Dinerstein, Joel. "The Soul Roots of Bruce Springsteen's American Dream." *American Music* 25 (2007): 441-476.

Duncan, Robert. "Lawdamercy, Springsteen Saves!." *Creem* October, 1978. Reprinted in Burger, *Springsteen on Springsteen*, 81-96.

Dunn, Mary Maples, and Richard S. Dunn. "The Founding: 1681-1701." *Philadelphia: A 300-Year History*. Edited by Russell Frank Weigley. New York and London: W.W. Norton, 1982. 1-32.

Evans, C. Stephen. *Faith Beyond Reason: A Kierkegaardian Account.* Grand Rapids, MI: Eerdmans, 1998.

Fishbane, Michael. *Biblical Text and Texture: A Literary Reading of Selected Texts.* New York: Schocken, 1979.

Forbes, Bruce David and Jeffrey H. Mahan, editors. *Religion and Popular Culture in America.* Berkeley and Los Angeles: University of California Press, 2005.

Gager, John G. *Reinventing Paul.* Oxford and New York: Oxford University Press, 2000.

García Martínez, Florentino and Eibert J. C. Tigchelaar, editors. *The Dead Sea Scrolls: Study Edition.* 2 Vols. Leiden: Brill, 1997.

Garman, Bryan K. *A Race of Singers: Whitman's Working-class Hero from Guthrie to Springsteen.* Chapel Hill: University of North Carolina Press, 2000.

Gill, Jerry H. "The Gospel According to Bruce." *Theology Today* 45 (1988): 87-94.

Gilmour, Michael J., editor. *Call Me the Seeker: Listening to Religion in Popular Music.* New York and London: Continuum, 2005.

Goodman, James. *But Where Is the Lamb?: Imagining the Story of Abraham and Isaac.* New York: Schocken, 2013.

Graybill, Mark S. "'As Empty as Paradise': Reading Religion in Bruce Springsteen's *The Rising.*" *Studies in American Culture* 33 (2010): 28-33.

Greeley, Andrew. "The Catholic Imagination of Bruce Springsteen." *America* 6 February, 1988: 232-243. Reprinted in Sawyers, *Racing in the Street: The Bruce Springsteen Reader*, 155-64.

Grossman, Maxine L. "Jesus, Mama, and The Constraints On Salvific Love in Contemporary Country Music." *Journal of the American Academy of*

Religion 70 (2002): 83-115. Reprinted in Gilmour, *Call Me the Seeker*, 267-298.

Hagen, Mark. "Meet the New Boss." *The Guardian* 17 Jan. 2009. Reprinted in Philips and Masur, *Talk about a Dream*, 355-364.

Harde, Roxanne. "'May Your Hope Give Us Hope': *The Rising* as a Site of Mourning." In Harde and Streight, *Reading the Boss*, 243-265.

Harde, Roxanne and Irwin Streight, editors. *Reading the Boss: Interdisciplinary Approaches to the Works of Bruce Springsteen*. Lanham, MD: Lexington, 2010. 151-173

Hartman, Geoffrey. "'*Was It for This* ...?' Wordsworth and the Birth of the Gods." *Romantic Revolutions: Criticism and Theory*. Edited by Kenneth R. Johnston, et al. Bloomington: Indiana University Press, 1990. 8-25.

Hartman, Lars. *'Into the Name of the Lord Jesus': Baptism in the Early Church*. Edinburgh: T & T Clark, 1997.

Helm, Paul. *Eternal God: A Study of God Without Time*. Oxford: Clarendon, 1988.

Henke, James. Interview with Bruce Springsteen. *Backstreets* 89, 2010. Reprinted in Philips and Masur, *Talk about a Dream*, 385-405.

Himmelfarb, Martha. *The Apocalypse: A Brief History*. Chichester, UK: Wiley-Blackwell, 2010.

Hoffman, Joel M. "Let Us Affirm the Holiness of the Day." *Who By Fire, Who By Water: U'ntanehTokef*. Edited by Lawrence A. Hoffman. Woodstock: Jewish Lights, 2010. 31-32.

Immanuel of Rome. "Eden and Hell." *The Penguin Book of Hebrew Verse*. Edited and translated by T. Carmi. New York: Penguin, 1981.

Jackson, Jerma A. *Singing in My Soul: Black Gospel Music in a Secular Age*. Chapel Hill: University of North Carolina Press, 2004.

Jindra, Michael. "It's About Faith in Our Future: Star Trek Fandom as Cultural Religion." In Forbes and Mahan, *Religion and Popular Culture in America*, 159-173.

John Paul II. *Ecclesia de Eucharistia* [Encyclical Letter On the Eucharist in its Relationship to the Church]. Accessed 3/23/2016. http://www.vatican.va/holy_father/special_features/encyclicals/documents/hf_jp-ii_enc_20030417_ecclesia_eucharistia_en.html

King, Karen L. "Jesus Said to Them, 'My Wife …': A New Coptic Papyrus Fragment." *Harvard Theological Review* 107 (2014): 131-59.

Kirkpatrick, Rob. *Magic in the Night: The Words and Music of Brice Springsteen.* New York: St. Martin's, 2009.

Knight, James. "'I Ain't Got No Home in This World Anymore': Protest and Promise in Woody Guthrie and the Jesus Tradition." In Gilmour, *Call Me the Seeker: Listening to Religion in Popular Music*, 17-33.

Kronfeld, Chana. *On the Margins of Modernism: Decentering Literary History.* Berkeley and Los Angeles: University of California Press, 1996.

Kronfeld, Chana. *The Full Severity of Compassion: The Poetry of Yehuda Amichai.* Stanford: Stanford University Press, 2016.

Kuebrich, David. "Religion and the Poet-Prophet." *A Companion to Walt Whitman.* Edited by Donald D. Kummings. Hoboken, NJ: Wiley, 2009. 197-215.

Kuebrich, David. *Minor Prophecy: Walt Whitman's New American Religion.* Bloomington: Indiana University Press, 1989.

Landau, Jon. "Growing Young with Rock and Roll." *The Real Paper* 20 March, 1974.

Lapsley, Jacqueline E. "'Bring On Your Wrecking Ball': Psalm 73 and Public Witness." *Theology Today* 70 (2013): 62-68.

Lawrence, D. H. "The Spirit of Place." *The Cambridge Edition of the Works of D. H. Lawrence*. Edited by Ezra Greenspan. Cambridge: Cambridge University Press, 2003.

Lewica, Michelle M. "Losing Their Way to Salvation: Women, Weight Loss, and the Salvation Myth of Culture Lite." In Forbes and Mahan, *Religion and Popular Culture in America*, 174-194.

Linkon, Sherry Lee, and John Russo. *Steeltown U.S.A.: Work and Memory in Youngstown*. Lawrence, KS: University of Kansas Press, 2002.

Loder, Kurt. "The Rolling Stone Interview: Bruce Springsteen." *Rolling Stone* 6 December, 1984. Reprinted in *Bruce Springsteen: The Rolling Stone Files*. New York: Hyperion, 1996. 151-165.

Marsh, Dave. *Glory Days: The Bruce Springsteen Story*. New York: Thunder's Mouth, 1996.

Masur, Louis P. *Runaway Dream:* Born to Run *and Bruce Springsteen's American Vision*. New York: Bloomsbury, 2009.

McCarthy, Kate. "Deliver Me from Nowhere: Bruce Springsteen and the Myth of the American Promised Land." *God in the Details: American Religion in Popular Culture*. Edited by Eric Michael Mazur and Kate McCarthy. New York and London: Routledge, 2000. 23-45.

Milosz, Czeslaw. "An Honest Description of Myself with a Glass of Whiskey at an Airport, Let Us Say, in Minneapolis." Translated by Robert Hass and Czeslaw Milosz. *New York Review of Books* 20 December, 2001.

Milosz, Czeslaw. *Second Space: New Poems*. Translated by Robert Haas. New York: Ecco, 2005.

Mornin, Edward, and Laura Mornin. *Saints: A Visual Guide*. Grand Rapids, MI: Eerdmans, 2006.

Moscheo, Joe, and Priscilla Beaulieu Presley. *The Gospel Side of Elvis*. New York: Center Street, 2007.

Moss, Pamela. "Still Searching for the Promised Land: Placing Women in Bruce Springsteen's Lyrical Landscapes." *Cultural Geographies* 18 (2011): 343-362.

Orel, Matthew. "From Adam to Jesus: Springsteen's Use of Scripture." In Womack, Zolten, and Bernhard, *Bruce Springsteen, Cultural Studies, and the Runaway American Dream*, 145-162.

Painter, John. *Just James: The Brother of Jesus in History and Tradition.* Minneapolis: Fortress, 1999.

Paley, Grace. *Begin Again: Collected Poems.* New York: Farrar, Straus & Giroux, 2001.

Percy, Will. Interview with Bruce Springsteen. *DoubleTake.* Spring, 1998. Reprinted in Philips and Masur, *Talk about a Dream*, 218-232.

Phillips, Chris. "*Born to Run*: The Lost Interviews: Part One." *Backstreets* 57 (1997). Reprinted in Phillips and Masur, *Talk About a Dream*, 30-55.

Price, Joseph L. "An American Apotheosis: Sports as Popular Religion." In Forbes and Mahan, *Religion and Popular Culture in America*, 195-212.

Randall, Linda K. *Finding Grace in the Concert Hall: Community and Meaning among Springsteen Fans.* Long Grove, IL: Waveland, 2011.

Rashkow, Ilona N. "Oedipus Wrecks: Moses and God's Rod." *Reading Bibles, Writing Bodies: Identity and the Book.* Edited by Timothy K. Beal and David Gunn. London: Routledge, 1997. 72-84.

Reed, Teresa L. *The Holy Profane: Religion in Black Popular Music.* Lexington: University of Kentucky Press, 2003.

Roberts, Chris. *Lou Reed: Walk on the Wild Side.* Milwaukee: Hal Leonard, 2004.

Rosen-Zvi, Ishay. *Demonic Desires:* Yetzer Hara *and the Problem of Evil in Late Antiquity.* Philadelphia: University of Pennsylvania Press, 2011.

Sasson, Jack M. *The Anchor Bible: Jonah*. New York: Doubleday, 1990.

Sawyers, June Skinner. "'Deliver Me from Nowhere': Spiritual Longing in the Music of Bruce Springsteen." Paper presented at *Glory Days: A Bruce Springsteen Symposium, Sept. 9th-11th, 2005*. West Long Beach, NJ.

Schor, Esther H. *Emma Lazarus*. New York: Schocken, 2006.

Sciaky, Ed. Interview with Bruce Springsteen. WMMR Radio; 3 November, 1974. Reprinted in Philips and Masur, *Talk about a Dream*, 21-29.

Seay, Devin, and Mary Neely. *Stairway to Heaven: The Spiritual Roots of Rock 'n' Roll—From the King and Little Richard to Prince and Amy Grant*. New York: Ballantine, 1986.

Shelley, Percy Bysshe, and Thomas J. Hogg. *The Necessity of Atheism*. Worthing: C. and W. Phillips, 1813

Shelley, Percy Bysshe. "A Defence of Poetry." *Shelley's Poetry and Prose*. Edited by Donald H. Reiman and Neil Fraistat. New York: Norton, 2002. 509-535.

Siker, John. "Yom Kippuring Passover: Recombinant Sacrifice in Early Christianity." *Ritual and Metaphor: Sacrifice in the Bible*. Edited by Christian A. Eberhart. Atlanta: Society of Biblical Literature, 2011. 65-82.

Springsteen, Bruce. Keynote Address. South by Southwest Music Festival. Austin, TX. 15 March, 2012. Reprinted in Burger, *Springsteen on Springsteen*, 384-398.

Springsteen, Bruce. *Songs*. HarperEntertainment, 2003.

Streight, Irwin. "The Ghost of Flannery O'Connor in the Songs of Bruce Springsteen." *Flannery O'Connor Review* 6 (2008): 11-15.

Streight, Irwin. "The Flannery O'Connor of American Rock." In Harde and Streight, *Reading the Boss*, 53-75.

Sutcliffe, Phil. "You Talkin' To Me?" *Mojo* January, 2006. Reprinted in Philips and Masur, *Talk about a Dream*, 300-319.

Symynkywicz, Jeffrey. *The Gospel According to Bruce Springsteen*. Louisville: Westminster John Knox, 2008.

Tennant, Frederick Robert. *The Sources of the Doctrines of the Fall and Original Sin*. New York: Schocken, 1968.

Till, Rupert. *Pop Cult: Religion and Popular Music*. London and New York: Continuum, 2010.

Tucker, Ken. Interview with Bruce Springsteen, *Entertainment Weekly* 28, February, 2003. Reprinted in Philips and Masur, *Talk about a Dream*, 271-280.

Turner, Steve. "Was Bob Dylan the Previous Bruce Springsteen?" *New Musical Express* 6 October, 1973. Reprinted in Burger, *Springsteen on Springsteen*, 8-12.

Turner, Steve. *Hungry for Heaven: Rock 'n' Roll and the Search for Redemption*. Downers Grove, IL.: InterVarsity, 1995.

Tyler, Andrew. "Bruce Springsteen and the Wall of Faith." *New Musical Express* November 15, 1975. Reprinted in Burger, *Springsteen on Springsteen*, 41-53.

Wager, Scott. "Life Right Now: Springsteen and Spirituality." In Womack, Zolten, and Bernhard, *Bruce Springsteen, Cultural Studies, and the Runaway American Dream*, 163-174.

Walter, Jennifer. "The Boss and the Bible: Biblical Imagery and the Spiritual Journey in the Songs of Bruce Springsteen." Paper presented at *Glory Days: A Bruce Springsteen Symposium, 9-11 September, 2005*. West Long Branch, NJ.

Warren, Bill. *I'll Take You There: Pop Music and the Urge for Transcendence*. New York: Continuum, 2005.

Whitman, Walt. *The Complete Poems of Walt Whitman*. Edited by Stephen Matterson. Hertfordshire: Wordsworth Poetry Library, 1995.

Wieder, Judy. Interview with Bruce Springsteen. *Advocate* 2 April, 1996. Reprinted in Philips and Masur, *Talk about a Dream*, 207-217.

Wimsatt, William K. and Monroe C. Beardsley. "The Intentional Fallacy." *Sewanee Review* 54 (1946): 468-88. Revised and reprinted in Wimsatt and Monroe, *The Verbal Icon: Studies in the Meaning of Poetry*. Lexington: University of Kentucky Press, 1954. 3-18.

Winston-Allen, Anne. *Stories of the Rose: The Making of the Rosary in the Middle Ages*. University Park: Pennsylvania State University Press, 1997.

Wolff, William. "Springsteen, Tradition, and the Purpose of the Artist." *BOSS: The Biannual Online-Journal of Springsteen Studies* 1 (2014): 36-73.

Womack, Kenneth, Jerry Zolten, and Mark Bernhard, editors. *Bruce Springsteen, Cultural Studies, and the Runaway American Dream*. Burlington: Ashgate, 2012

Yadin, Azzan and Ghil'ad Zuckermann. "Blorit: Pagan Mohawk or Sabra Forelock?: Ideologically Manipulative Secularization of Hebrew Terms in Socialist Zionist Israel." *The Sociology of Language and Religion: Change, Conflict, and Accommodation*. Edited by Tope Omoniyi. London and New York: Palgrave Macmillan, 2009. 84-124.

Yadin, Azzan and Samuel Moyn. "The Creaturely Limits of Knowledge: Martin Heidegger's Theological Critique of Immanuel Kant." *The Weimar Moment: Political Theology, Liberalism, and the Law*. Edited by Leonard V. Kaplan and Rudy Koshar. Lanham, MD: Lexington Books, 2012. 123-144.

Yadin, Azzan. "A Measure of Beauty." *Jewish Review of Books* 3 (2010): 44-45.

Yadin, Azzan. "Web of Chaos: Bialik and Nietzsche on Language, Truth and the Death of God." *Prooftexts* 21 (2001): 179-203

Yamin, George Y., Jr. "The Theology of Bruce Springsteen." *Journal of Religious Studies* 16 (1990): 1-21.

Young, Dean. "Scarecrow on Fire." *Fall Higher*. Port Townsend, WA: Copper Canyon, 2011.

Zitelli, Lisa. "'Like a Vision She Dances': Re-Visioning the Female Figure in the Songs of Bruce Springsteen." In Harde and Streight, *Reading the Boss*, 151-173.

Index of Bruce Springsteen Songs

www.ingramcontent.com/pod-product-compliance
Ingram Content Group UK Ltd.
Pitfield, Milton Keynes, MK11 3LW, UK
UKHW020142250726
13967UKWH00002B/815